Self-Discipline

This book includes:

Self-Discipline Mastery
&
Overthinking.

Self-Development Workbook to Master Self-Confidence, Reach Goals and Build Success With a Relentless Mindset.

Table of Contents

Self-Discipline Mastery

Control your mind, build willpower & master your mindset.

Learn habits to overcome procrastination, increase self-confidence and develop mental toughness.

Introduction

How many times have you told yourself, "I will worry about it tomorrow" or "I can´t go to the gym today, I just don't have the energy"? Have you ever had two weeks to finish a project, but you´ve been chilling 12 days and on the thirteenth day you started to freak out you don´t have enough time to do the work properly? How many times have you told to yourself, "If only I had better self-discipline, I wouldn't procrastinate so much"?

Life puts obstacles and difficulties in your way to success, and to stand above them, you must work with determination and confidence. This, of course, requires self-discipline. The mastery of this skill leads to self-confidence and self-esteem, and hence to happiness and satisfaction with your work and life. On the other hand, the lack of self-discipline may lead to failure, destruction, well-being or relationships' problems, health problems, etc.

For many people, self-discipline represents a genuine and allusive attribute that often slips through their fingertips. There is a plenitude of fields in our daily life where many of us want to do better.

This fact is especially obvious according to the millions of people making the New Year's resolutions every year. All those resolutions usually involve goals associated with losing weight, creating a healthier lifestyle, saving more money and improving the financial status, relationships and the elimination of bad habits (i.e., smoking, drinking, etc.).

However, less than 10% of these resolutions are observed. The main reason why it's like that is that people set either too many, or too unrealistic goals to achieve. Also, they may be victims of so called "false hope syndrome", which is defined as a person's unrealistic expectations about the possible speed, amount, ease and consequences of changing their behavior.

For many people, it requires a radical change in their attitude. It may take medical diagnosis to make you give up alcohol and it may require pregnancy to give up smoking. To transform your common behavior, you first have to change your thinking.

This book is all about learning tips and strategies to help you strengthen your self-discipline so you can focus on your tasks and become successful.

My aim in this book is to give you the tools you need to become mentally tough and so you can master your self-discipline. It won't be the easiest journey that you take in your life, but it is one of the most rewarding and helpful journeys that will keep you going. It will strengthen your confidence, which will make you believe in yourself. You will learn what you are truly capable of accomplishing and this is something that money cannot buy. Your time is now. Maybe you have been thinking about improving your self-discipline for years. Now you´re in the right place to take control of your life. Stop allowing your inner critic and other negative thoughts to take over. It is time to truly know what you are capable of and reach for the stars.

Part 1: Theory

"Self-discipline is often disguised as short-term pain, which often leads to long-term gains. The mistake many of us make is the need and want for short-term gains (immediate gratification), which often leads to long-term pain."

— Charles F. Glassman

Chapter 1: Conquer Your Mind, Conquer the World

You are here because you want to improve your life. You might want to focus more on the tasks you need to complete at work. You might feel that your life needs more of a balance between work, time with your family, friends, and time for yourself. You might also be here because you want to improve your mindset by focusing on your self-discipline. No matter why you choose this book, the first step to mastering your self-discipline is understanding what it is and how to start developing it. The first step in this process is to start conquering your mind as this will allow you to conquer your world.

When I talk about conquering your world, I mean the world around you—the parts of the world you can control. The pieces of this include your mind, emotions, and actions. You can't control what other people do, say, or think. However, you can control how you react to other people's attitudes and actions.

Understanding Self-Discipline

People often struggle with self-discipline because they must step out of their comfort zone to improve themselves. It is a working progress that you will focus on every day of your life. You won't be perfect at it every day, but you will always do your best, and this is exactly what you need to do. It is always important to take the success along with the failures as this shows your progress.

What Is Self-Discipline

"Self-discipline is the magic power that makes you virtually unstoppable."

- Anonymous

Self-discipline is controlling your own thoughts, emotions, actions, and desires through self-improvement methods. The goal is that you will focus on developing your self-discipline by trying to better yourself every day. Learning self-discipline is not easy, but you will quickly notice the benefits and strive to better yourself in order to keep those benefits in your life.

Many people see self-discipline as an uneasy and difficult road to follow. As someone who has worked on developing their self-discipline for years, I will admit it is not easy. There are days where you find yourself struggling more than most to stay in your disciplined mindset. However, once you gain the willpower, you will find a strategy that works for you. You will find yourself practicing self-discipline throughout your day. It will become a natural part of your routine.

Self-discipline is not denying yourself life's pleasures. It is not making sure you always walk in a straight line along your life's path. There are always bumps, curves, and even some potholes that you need to navigate and that might take you a bit off course. Self-discipline is a pleasant experience that you will find achievable. You will start to notice some of the benefits within days of working on your self-discipline, which will start to keep you more focused. In many ways, self-discipline is part of the puzzle of your life. Sometimes you lose the pieces and you need to look for them, sometimes they are right in front of your face, and other times it seems they fall from the sky and directly into place.

Self-discipline is one of the most important life skills for people to develop. Many people, especially those who have mastered self-discipline, compare it to a superpower because it allows you to remain mindful of your actions, thoughts, and emotions.

Mindfulness is when you are aware of everything going on in your environment — especially yourself. You notice if you ate enough, you know when you start to feel overwhelmed, when your thoughts are negative, or when you are tired and need to rest. Mindfulness and self-discipline go together, you cannot have one without the other. This is because the opposite of mindfulness is mindlessness, which is when you are not aware of your environment, thoughts, emotions, and actions. Take a moment to think about when you are driving your regular route to work, the grocery store, or your friend's house. You are used to the scenery and know exactly where you are going, so you let your mind wander. When you park your vehicle, you ask yourself how you got there because you don't remember part of the route. This is an example of becoming mindless. If you are mindful, you would remember everything about your drive.

Developing Your Self-Discipline

The most critical part of reaching your goals is developing your self-discipline. The struggle people tend to have is the resistance they feel pulling them away from their self-discipline. For example, you started a new diet last week and are struggling to stay away from the food you love but can't have. Even though you threw away all the food in your home that you aren't allowed to eat on the diet, you continue to see the food everywhere. Potato chips, which are your favorite snacks, are not acceptable on this diet. You have been craving potato chips for several days and are not sure how much longer you can stay away from your favorite snack. Your mind keeps telling you, "Just a few won't hurt you; buy a small bag and go for a long walk in the morning." After a few more days, you decide to have a cheat day and feed your cravings. You tell yourself, "It will be better tomorrow. Besides, I have had a tough week, and everyone deserves a cheat day now and then."

It is the belief in cheat days that lead people to lose their self-discipline when they start a diet. It is the thoughts you have that tell you, "It is okay to have a few cookies, as long as you don't do it every day" that keeps you from strengthening your self-discipline.

There are dozens of ways you can develop your self-discipline. You don't have to follow the path that other people have taken — you can develop your own plan and what works for your lifestyle and personality. In fact, you are more likely to succeed on your self-discipline journey if you develop your own path based on what you need.

Before I take you further into your self-development journey, it is important that you understand these tips that will help you master your self-discipline.

1. **Set clear goals.** One of the biggest reasons people struggle with self-discipline is because they do not establish clear goals. They have an idea of the goal they want to reach, but they don't think about the process of this goal. They don't form steps that will help them remain focused on their goals.

2. **Create a backup plan.** A backup plan will help you through a difficult time or a moment when you find a fault in your original plan. Backup plans don't mean that you must stop focusing on your original plan, they simply mean that you will help yourself through the bumps in your path.

3. **Know your weaknesses.** Your weaknesses are nothing to be ashamed of as everyone has weaknesses just like everyone has strengths. The key is to understand your weaknesses as this will guide you to know what direction you need to take on the path to reach your self-discipline. The only way you will overcome your weakness is by admitting you have them.

4. **Keep your new habits simple.** Trying to follow a new habit can be a daunting task because it is hard to break your old habits. One way to keep yourself from feeling intimidated is to create simple new habits. For example, if you want to start working out for an hour every day to lose weight and get in shape, you will begin by exercising 15 minutes a day. Once you become more motivated to exercise, add 5 to 10 minutes onto your time. Slowly increase your time until you are exercising for an hour a day.

5. **Believe you have willpower.** When people believe they have willpower, they believe they can achieve their goals. They will continue to build their motivation to succeed, which starts to increase your self-esteem and self-image. This helps you become a more positive person and continues to keep you motivated, even when you hit the bumps in the road.

6. **Learn from your mistakes.** You will stumble from time to time, no matter how strong your self-discipline becomes. You can establish the best steps to reach your goals and still find yourself struggling. This happens to everyone and it is important to not let it get you down. Acknowledge what happened and continue to move forward. When you start letting yourself feel angry or

guilty, you will continue to struggle and slow down your progress. You can't succeed without failure.

7. **Reward yourself.** One of the important steps in establishing your goals is making sure you set rewards for yourself. You want to treat yourself in a way that will keep you motivated to continue. For example, you might watch an episode of your favorite show on Netflix, go to the movies with a friend, or go out to eat.

Self-Confidence Vs. Self-Esteem

As an entrepreneur, Roger has recently learned he needs to work on self-improvement by taking control of his self-discipline. A couple of months ago, Roger started his own writing business where he works for several clients as a writer and editor. Recently, Roger started to notice that he is not following his schedule, he is easily distracted, and he doesn't always have the willpower to sit at his desk and work. Roger knows that he doesn't lack the motivation for his work or lost interest in his job. He enjoys writing and has put in a lot of work over the last few years to establish his business.

Roger first realized his struggles getting into his schedule within his first week of working from home. At this time, Roger contributed his struggles to years of stress working two jobs. Not only did Roger focus on developing his business, but he also worked full-time as a journalist. His job often caused him to work more than 40 hours a week and odd hours as he had to cover evening and weekend events. This caused him to lack a schedule with both jobs. Furthermore, Roger worked close to 100 hours a week for over six months. These factors made Roger think he was dealing with the aftereffects of eliminating a huge amount of stress from his shoulders. He talked to His friends about his struggles and they agreed that in a couple of weeks, Roger would start to focus more on his schedule and continue to build his business. But, almost two months later, Roger is still struggling.

Roger has an idea of what self-discipline is but doesn't have a clear idea of how to effectively reach self-discipline. He has never focused on improving his self-discipline and is not sure of the steps he will need to take. Roger starts to do a little research about self-discipline and how he can incorporate its strategies into his life so he will have more motivation to follow his schedule and complete his tasks. The first point Roger learns is that he is already improving because he understands that he needs to work on his self-discipline.

Roger is already improving because he acknowledges his weaknesses and wants to focus on establishing good self-discipline strategies so he can continue to grow his business and general self-improvement.

One of the first factors Roger realized about himself is his low self-confidence. He didn't realize all the negative thoughts he had throughout the day. He didn't notice how often he questioned his abilities as a writer and editor. Even though his clients loved his work, he continued to believe that his talent could vanish in an instant. He felt that his clients would find someone better and his business would fail. Roger realized that he needed to change his mindset to gain a stronghold of his self-discipline.

One day at a time, Roger started building his plan to take control of his emotions and thoughts. He used strategies to become more mindful and started reflecting on his day through journaling for 15 minutes before he went to bed. In the morning, he got up a half-hour early and started to meditate before getting ready for the day. He started to eat healthier, focusing on smaller meals and eating more often. Roger started snacking on healthy foods over cookies, chips, and candy. He gave up soda, started drinking more water, and go at least 7 hours of sleep every night. Over time, Roger started to feel better emotionally, mentally, and physically.

Like Roger, you don't think about self-discipline because you become comfortable with your daily routine and habits. They become a part of your life and that is just the way it is. Another reason you don't spend a lot of thought on self-discipline is because of your low self-confidence.

It is important to understand the difference between self-confidence and self-esteem. You can have high self-esteem and still have low self-confidence. Your self-esteem is how you feel about yourself overall. You focus on the positive experiences that have happened throughout your life, giving you a positive outlook. Self-confidence is how you feel about your abilities and talents. You might think that your artwork or writing is never good enough or that you aren't good at math. However, you will feel that you are strong in other areas, such as interior decorating. Self-confidence can change from one situation to the next.

When you start observing yourself in the mission to increase your self-discipline, you will notice that you have high self-confidence where your self-discipline is strong. When your self-discipline is weak, your self-confidence is also weak. Your self-discipline follows how confident you feel about certain situations. To help you understand, think about a skill you have that you feel you aren't good at. How motivated are you when it comes to focusing on that skill? For example, if you feel you aren't a good artist, you won't spend a lot of time drawing or painting. But, if your confidence is high as an artist, you are motivated to work on your projects often. If you need to, take some time to write down skills you are confident about and skills where your self-confidence is low. Then, take a moment to think about how motivated you are to focus on these skills. Write down how you feel about the skills and think of ways in which you can start to build your self-confidence, thus building your self-discipline in these skills.

You need to remember that self-discipline is a skill, which is something that you learn over time. Developing your self-discipline takes time, patience, and commitment. You will find yourself feeling like you can't build your self-discipline and you will have days where you are strong in this area of your life. Everything you feel as you work towards strengthening your self-discipline is normal. In the moments where you start to question yourself, take a moment to think about what you have accomplished. Above all, you always need to remember that you are on the right path and you are doing a great job. You are not alone in this struggle. Always be proud of your improvements.

Chapter 2: Mindset

The key to improving your self-discipline is your mindset. This is something that I had to learn by myself, which is something I want to make easier for you. I felt alone as I knew I needed to change the way I felt about myself and this made my journey even harder. Once I realized that I wasn't alone, that there were thousands of other people trying to change their mindset, I started to grow a little by little each day.

I didn't receive a lot of support as a child. I remember coming home at the age of 12 to my parents laughing at a story I had written. As a child, writing was a way to escape the struggles I faced daily. When my parents found my notebook and made fun of everything, I lost all confidence in my ability as a growing writer. I stopped writing for many years and started to keep to myself more. I couldn't find a different way to work through my thoughts and emotions, so they continued to pile up inside of me. Eventually, they became unbearable. However, I continued to remain quiet because I didn't want to cause a scene. I didn't want people to start thinking I was crazy or couldn't control myself.

I was in my third year of college and about to flunk out when a professor reached out to me. He told me what a gift I had for writing and how much he enjoyed reading my papers. I didn't know what to say, other than "thank you" so I just stood there awkwardly. I left his classroom thinking that he would change his mind the next time. After all, I had no talent for writing.

He never changed his mind. In fact, more professors started to talk to me about my papers and told me I should think about taking technical and creative writing courses to expand my writing. Finally, I opened to one of my professors and told him that I wasn't going to work on my writing because it really wasn't that good and eventually, he would believe it too. I will never forget how his mouth dropped and how quickly he shook his head. He then told me, "No, you just don't realize how good you are, yet. Come to my office tomorrow after class as I want to show you something."

The next day I followed him back to his office, he had me sit beside him on his couch and told me that I was going to learn how to meditate. He told me about his childhood struggles and how meditation was his first step to changing his mindset. For three days every week, I went to his office and we spent 10 minutes meditating.

After a couple of weeks, he gave me an inspirational book of quotes. He told me to read one quote every time I noticed a negative thought or feeling. He also gave me a journal and told me to start writing about my day before I went to bed every night. I could write about how I felt during certain situations and how I changed my negative thoughts into positive thoughts.

As the weeks went by, I gradually started to focus more on positivity. I found myself reading an inspirational quote and listening to a motivational video on YouTube every morning. When I struggled during the day, I would take out my book of quotes and read one.

A decade later, and I now believe I am a talented writer. Of course, I still have my days where my mindset is a bit weaker. These days, I focus more on the strategies I have learned throughout these last few years to gain more confidence and refocus my mindset.

I didn't realize until I noticed my own teenage son struggling with his mindset after dealing with bullying in school that changing our mindset is a choice. It wasn't that I couldn't change my mindset as a teenager or without the help of my professor, it was that I didn't truly understand and didn't believe I could. It was my choice to continue focusing on the negativity in my life. This is now something that I am trying to teach my teenager — you need to say 'yes' and know what you really want.

Fixed and Growth Mindset

As you can see from my story, changing your mindset will not happen overnight. It is a process that you will spend years on. In fact, you will focus on growing your mindset for the rest of your life. This doesn't mean every day will be one struggle after another where you will need to take time for yourself and focus on the positives over the negatives. You will have days when you feel choosing your positive mindset over the negative is natural and days where you need to work at it a little more.

It Is Always Your Choice

After years of focusing on developing a more positive and calmer mindset, I still have days where I need to choose to spend more time on the positives than negatives. There are days where I am lacking energy and feel that lying in bed thinking about my bad day is the best option. However, I know that always focusing on growing and fixing my mindset is completely up to me. So, what do I do? I accept my bad day and focus on the happy moments. I take my moment where I sit in the dark and reflect on the negative parts of my day.

Then, I start to focus on the positives. I start at the beginning and think about how my family is healthy and happy. I focus on my job and how much I enjoy what I do. I think about all the progress I have made on my mindset over the last few years. Slowly, my mindset begins to change. I start to feel that this day is one day. It doesn't define who I am.

It is easy to get 'down in the dumps' when you are having a bad day. There are days when climbing out of the dumps is easier and some days when it is harder. There are days where opening your inspirational book of quotes will not help like it normally does and this can make you feel worse. In these moments, you need to continue to focus on your strategies to grow your mindset. The key to remember in these moments is how you respond to your mindset is *your choice*. Ask yourself, "Am I going to sit here and feel bad for myself or am I going to pick myself up, dust myself off, and start fresh?" Remember you can start fresh at any moment throughout your day.

Fixed Mindset

A fixed mindset is one of the two main types of mindsets people have. A fixed mindset is when you don't focus on growing your mindset through strategies. When you have a fixed mindset, you believe your abilities are fixed within you and cannot change. This means that you won't work to improve your mindset because you don't believe it is possible. A fixed mindset doesn't mean you have low self-confidence or self-esteem. You value your worth and you know what you can achieve, but you don't believe you can go beyond what you believe is set for you.

A fixed mindset means that you believe your talent is what will bring you to success. You won't reach success by working hard or putting more effort into your career. For example, you tell yourself that you are good or something or you're not. You believe that even if you try to accomplish a task that you aren't good at, you will fail. Therefore, you don't believe in wasting your time trying to achieve a new task. Instead, you continue to focus on what you are good at. Another example of a fixed mindset is refusing to learn anything new because you already know everything you need to know.

You might have developed your fixed mindset because of the way you were raised, or you were told that you couldn't improve. For example, you decided to pick up the flute for a band in school. You practiced often and found yourself as one of the top flute players. While you continue to practice, your parents and band instructor started to tell you that you can't get any better as a flute player. You were already the first chair and took the lead in programs. Because of this, you started to feel stuck and didn't think there was another goal for you as a flute player. Therefore, you developed a fixed mindset when it came to play the flute.

Growth Mindset

A growth mindset is the opposite of a fixed mindset. If you have a growth mindset, you believe that you can continue to learn and improve over time. In fact, you believe that you can always improve your mindset if you work on it. There is always time to learn something new and give yourself better opportunities.

If you have a fixed mindset, it is possible to develop a growth mindset. Carol Dweck, Professor of Psychology at Stanford University, wrote a book titled *Mindset: The New Psychology of Success* where she talks about growth and fixed mindsets in depth. Through her research, Dweck described the fixed and growth mindset. Since then, several psychologists and other researchers have worked on strategies to transform your fixed mindset to a growth mindset.

- **See challenges as opportunities.** You face challenges every day. You might have to find the answer to a difficult question, such as whether you should take a new job, or faced with accomplishing a new task at work. If you see challenges as a roadblock, it is time to view them as an opportunity for growth. Take time to think about how you can grow with the challenge and visualize yourself overcoming this challenge.

- **Never stop learning.** You might not be in school anymore, but this doesn't mean you stop learning. You can continue to learn every day by reading and learning new tasks. Learning will help you understand that your brain is constantly learning new information which helps it grow.

- **Needing to improve does not mean you are a failure.** Needing to improve in any area of your life doesn't mean you are failing. It means that you still have room for growth and to become your best self.

- **Don't be afraid of failure.** Failure doesn't mean that you can't do something, it means that you need to try again. Learn from your mistakes and move on. Think of failure as an opportunity to establish more strengths in your life.

- **Learn well, not fast.** There is a difference between learning something well and learning it quickly. Even if you feel you need to learn your new task quickly, it is more important that you understand the steps of your task. You want to perform your work well and not quickly.

To Learn or Not to Learn?

Part of your self-discipline mastery is to achieve the mindset that learning is living. You want to make learning a priority as this will open your mind to all areas of your life. It will give you more motivation to continue building your self-discipline. Learning also helps you manage your self-discipline because you become more aware of your actions and emotions.

Most people think they can only learn in school. They believe that learning comes from the classroom. This isn't true. In fact, you are learning right and probably not sitting in a classroom as you are reading this book.

To make learning a priority in your life, you need to keep your eyes and ears open. You need to focus when you are learning and note it within your mind. The more interested you are in what you are learning, the more you will remember it. If you are learning something new by reading a book and move on to another activity without giving what you have learned another thought, you will not remember it.

Understand the World

You need to look around your environment. You need to understand what is going on. For example, if you are walking down the street and you see someone who looks like they could be homeless on the corner of the street with a sign. As you walk closer, you see the sign reads, "Anything will help." The sign tugs at your heartstrings as you begin to realize there are holes in the person's shoes. You see their hair is a mess and they are not clean. You then notice all the cars driving by. Some people stare at the person while others act like they don't notice anyone is standing there.

You walk up to the person and give them what little cash you had in your pocket. They tell you, "Thank you so much. God bless you." You are about to walk away but then stop and think you want to know more. You want to know why the person is in this situation. You want to know if they know of any resources around the area. You want to know whatever information they can give you because you want to try to help not only this person but every homeless person in your area. While you don't live in a large city, you know there are several resources for the homeless in your city and all of them struggle to help everyone on the streets. This tells you that there is a lack of help for the homeless in your area. You turn around and ask if the person will talk to you for a bit over a meal. They agree and you head to the local restaurant.

As you are about to walk in you notice that the person, who has recently introduced themselves to you as Sam set their cart directly in front of the window. They then ask you, "Would you mind if we sit right there so I can watch my stuff. It's all I have." You agree as you open the door.

When you have a mission to help the homeless, one of the best ways to learn how to get into the nonprofit world to help them is by talking to people. You want to talk to the homeless people in your area and to any other nonprofits that aim to help the homeless. Talk to as many people and organizations that you can so you can get a clear and thorough understanding. You might find that while there are plenty of places homeless people can get food and clothing, there aren't enough places in the area that can offer them a place to sleep. Therefore, you learn that what your community really needs is a nonprofit that will help with this resource. You might discover that you not only have a place that offers a few beds, but you work with churches in the area to create more space for them to sleep, especially when the nights are cold.

Teach Other People About Your World

Another part of learning is to teach other people about your world. You want to take action for what you have learned as this will further your understanding. At the same time, you need to realize there are different ways to understand the concept. For instance, people will understand homelessness differently from you. Some people may have found themselves homeless for a period of time and this gives them a different view. Other people may have helped someone only to find out that they were scamming for money and now have a sour point of view about homeless people.

You need to become open to your experiences and have patience when you are talking to other people. At the same time, you also need to understand their experiences and what they feel about the situation you are discussing. For example, if a person brushes you off because they don't believe homelessness is a problem in the community, you can show them statistics instead of talking about your experience.

Treat Learning as an Inspiration

There are two ways that you can learn. You can learn on autopilot or you can become interested in what you are learning. When you become interested, you will feel inspired. You will want to learn as much as you can and help other people understand what you have learned. Treating learning as an inspiration will allow you to focus on the quality throughout the project.

Learning Helps Your Mindset Grow

You can't continue to grow your mindset without learning. You need to focus on your task, your environment, and listen to other people in order to have a growth mindset. This is because, with a growth mindset, you focus on progress and look for opportunities to help expand your knowledge and abilities. For example, Roger soon started to learn about the opportunities writing had for him — opportunities he never thought of until he started his writing business and started to gain the self-confidence he needed to develop as a writer.

One of the factors Roger learned that he loved to focus on as a writer was helping other writers. He believed in his talent and started to open up to other writers about how he develops, the mindset he uses, and how he starts his writing process. Over time, Roger started to notice that other writers came to him for advice. This quickly became one of Roger's favorite tasks. He wanted to help other writers develop.

As Roger started researching what other job opportunities were available for him as a writer, he came across the opportunity to be a writing coach. Looking more into this job, he noted that it was what he enjoyed doing the most. He looked at the qualification for a certificate and decided that he would save a little money from each of his paychecks to pay for the certification. Roger established becoming a writing coach as a goal and developed the steps to ensure he would reach his goal within two years.

Chapter 3: Key to Success

Think back to when you were a child and how you viewed the world. How you looked at the world and learned about everything around you depends on how far back you remember. For example, if you remember being a small child, you might remember feeling that everything was new to you. Your mind was busy trying to learn everything that you come across every day. If you remember the age of 9, you probably only learned because of school. You didn't care to learn too much outside of school, at least for the most part. Instead, you liked to relax and spend more time doing the activities you enjoyed. As a teenager, your interest in learning subsided. It felt more like a job you had to do when you would rather sit at home and watch television or play video games.

At least if you are like Drake, you don't care to learn much as a teenager. Drake's mother, Amirah, didn't understand what had happened to her son's grades. He used to receive A's and B's. Sometimes his grades would drop down to a C, but he could bring it back up quickly. Since the age of 12, Amirah has noticed her son's grades are lower. He usually struggles to keep his grades at C's and has more D's. This quarter, he even has an F, which he has never received before. Amirah and her husband have worked with the school to make sure their son has everything he needs, they help him with his homework, at least when he brings it home.

Amirah has tried to talk to Drake countless times about his grades and what he needs. However, he always tells her that he doesn't know what is going on or the work isn't interesting. In the middle of the first quarter, Amirah realized she had to limit her son's screen time more because he would lie about any homework so he could play his games or watch television. She felt that making sure he had time to do any homework, even if it was only reading, would help. Unfortunately, Drake continues to struggle with his grades.

But, it's not just school that Drake doesn't have an interest in when it comes to learning. He would rather not do any type of learning. He used to love going to museums and learning about different cultures and topics with his mom, but he doesn't care to do any of these activities anymore. At one time, Amirah worried her son was depressed. However, the therapist informed her that Drake just isn't interested in learning like he used to be, and this is normal for many kids. "Some children just stop caring about learning when they become preteens or teenagers. As long as you continue to focus on the value of education, Drake will come around. He still has goals of going to college, which is good. This is only a phase and nothing really to worry about. Do what you can to get him to keep his grades up and work on his homework. If you find himself struggling more, come back and I will see if there is anything else, I can do."

Not every child is like Drake. There are many kids who thrive on learning throughout their life. However, some children would rather start to focus on something else than what they are learning. One reason for this is because if they aren't interested in it, they don't want to learn it. Another reason children stop willing to learn at a certain age is they lack motivation. Some children stop learning because they don't understand the value of education. Sometimes the child's role model is the reason they don't want to learn anymore. They feel that if their parents don't focus on learning, why should they? Another reason is that they might feel the task is too hard. They might have anxiety or give up easily because they don't think they can complete the task.

No matter what the reason for your child's disinterest in learning, it is up to you to do what you can to help them through this process calmly and rationally. Realize that you can talk until you are blue in the face and they might not take another step into learning. You can explain how important their grades are for college, but they might not want to go to college. In reality, it is difficult to get your child to learn when they don't care to do so. Sometimes taking away their phones or gaming privileges doesn't help as much as you thought it would.

Motivated to Learn

You don't have to be a preteen or teenager to become unmotivated to learn. There are students who are in their third year of college and find themselves becoming less focused on learning. Some people struggle with learning once they graduate from college and become comfortable in their job. They don't feel that learning is a part of their lifestyle anymore. Whatever your age or reasoning for losing your motivation to learn, there are several strategies you can follow to change your habits and focus more on learning. After all, you won't reach your self-discipline mastery without learning every day.

- **Take the time to read every day.** You don't have to spend a lot of time reading, but it should be enjoyable. Don't force yourself to read a book that you aren't interested in. You can include reading as part of your daily routine. For example, get up half an hour earlier every morning and read. If it's your child, who is struggling with learning, find a book that they will be interested in and include them in this process. It doesn't matter if your child focuses on reading a comic book, as long as they are reading you are helping them increase their willingness to learn.

- **Focus on interests.** There will always be topics you are not interested in learning. Your child is always going to have subjects in school that they struggle with because 'math isn't their thing'. This is okay, it is a part of life. Of course, you don't want to allow them to have bad grades but understand that this subject is harder for them because they aren't interested. Instead of focusing on what isn't interesting, you want to focus on what is. For example, if your child is interested in video games, encourage them to explore the ways video games are created.

- **Learn something new every day.** Take time every day to talk to your child about something new that you learned. Ask them to share something that they learned throughout the day. This can be anything they learned; it doesn't have to be a part of their school day. Encourage them to explore more about the world around them and show them that you will do the same.

- **Watch videos.** At the end of the day, you're not limited anymore to only read books like your parents and grandparent were. Use the digital age and explore from the thousands of the educative videos on the internet about any topic you can think of. If you´re willing to incorporate more learning into your daily routine and you can´t fit reading a book In your schedule, watch a video or listen to a podcast while you walk to work, gym or on a treadmill in the gym.

Grow Your Mental Toughness

What is meant by growing your mental toughness? It means that you learn to resist and overcome your concerns, worries, doubts, and anything or anyone that keeps you from succeeding. Your mindset becomes tough as you realize no one can tell you what your self-worth is — you are the only person who knows your self-worth.

Mental toughness means that you need to work on your growth mindset consciously, but you also need to focus on this in steps. The first step is to master your mindset. This means you have to take in all the theories you have read through this book and apply them to your life. The next part will help you work through the steps to develop your mindset, mental toughness, and achieve your self-discipline mastery.

Mental toughness does not mean that you are self-absorbed and don't notice what other people say about you. It doesn't mean that you are unemotional. Mental toughness doesn't mean that you don't appreciate people or that you are unkind. People who have mental toughness are very compassionate, understanding, and willing to help other people at a moment's notice. Mental toughness does not mean you are physically tough as it has nothing to do with your physical strength. It focuses on your emotional and mental strength. While you want to have a positive mindset, mental toughness is not all about positive thinking. It is about being realistic and rational in your thinking. It is about maintaining a clear mind. Mental toughness is a mindset that leads you to success because you won't let failure or roadblocks stop you. You are self-confident in your abilities and you know your self-worth. Mental toughness is the mind of an entrepreneur — someone who understands that people will say hurtful statements about them or their company, but also understands that this does not define their business. What defines their business is their actions, the actions of their employees, and how they handle criticism.

Mental toughness is a skill that you will help you in all areas of your life. For example, Roger finds himself quickly losing self-confidence as he deals with tough editors and clients who are harsh when it comes to the work Roger gives them. He tries to tell himself that revisions are part of the job for a ghostwriter. He understands that some clients don't give him enough information for the outline but have a very specific idea about what they want. However, this doesn't keep Roger from feeling a little disappointed in himself when he is given a revision.

While Roger is talking to one of his co-workers, they tell him that he needs to develop a mentally tough attitude with the ghostwriting business. As Roger continues to develop this attitude, he finds himself showing more leadership and confidence in other areas of his life, such as when he is volunteering for a local nonprofit or coaching soccer. He finds himself becoming more driven to learn and spending less time in front of the television.

Core Distinctions of Mental Toughness

- **Prepared.** A mentally tough individual is prepared for anything that could happen. You develop a plan of action for your goals and often a backup plan.
- **Winning mindset.** Your winning mindset is the attitude you have whether you win or lose in a game or find yourself accomplishing or failing at a task. This mindset is the belief that you will succeed. It is a mindset that is solid and doesn't waver.
- **Focused.** You find yourself peaking with your best performance and don't allow yourself to become distracted. You keep your mind clear and many people state that you get "into the zone" when you are working on a task.

- **Stress management.** You can handle stress well. Even when your job becomes stressful, you remain focused and you don't allow stress to affect you in your job or your professional life. You understand that part of succeeding is stress and you need to experience this part of the job to understand what you can truly accomplish.

Mental toughness is the part of your mindset that you will develop constantly. Even when you feel like you have reached your maximum toughness, you will continue to work on its development as you are always working on your mindset.

Benefits of Mental Toughness

Mental toughness is a newer phenomenon in the world, but one that is quickly becoming popular because of its benefits.

- You will focus more on helpful advice and tune out advice that won't help you along your journey.
- You will feel more motivated to continue your journey, even when you run into negativity, whether this is a negative review of your business or people who don't support you.
- You will handle negative reviews in a more rational way. You will look at what the reviewer says and at the source of the review. You will note if the reviewer is logical with their

judgment or not. If they are not, you will find yourself moving on from the situation. If they are, you will take their review as advice and incorporate it into your business or other area of your life.

• You gain the courage to face your fears through mental toughness. You become more comfortable with stepping outside of your comfort zone. You understand that feeling uncomfortable leads you to success.

• You are more in control of your emotions through mental toughness. You think rationally about the situation in front of you and don't make decisions based on your emotions.

• You bounce back from failure quickly. You see failure as a learning opportunity and are ready to persevere and reach the next stage in your life.

One of the best benefits of mental toughness, is you don't let people take control of your career or your life. You develop a tough mind that allows you to stay on the right track to reach success. Even if it is your friends or family members trying to push you off track, you will find yourself overcoming their push and pull to focus on what is best for you. You will learn to let go of the people who don't support you and focus on the people who do.

An example of the growth of mental toughness and how it affects you in your personal and professional life comes from a young woman named Amirah. She grew up in a home that many people would call average. She felt unappreciated by her parents. She never felt truly loved by them because they pushed her to the side. They focused more on what they wanted than on what she needed. It didn't matter if she brought good or bad grades home from school, her parents didn't respond in any way. There were times she had to forge her mother's signature on school papers because her parents weren't home to sign the papers or refused because it was a waste of their time.

With the help of her high school guidance counselor and teachers, Amirah applied for college, received financial aid, and started her freshman year hours away from her parents. Amirah decided that at the start of her college years she would focus on herself. She didn't need her parents for anything. She would find new friends and establish a new family.

Amirah didn't understand what mental toughness was until she took a general psychology course. It was at that moment Amirah realized that she not only had to work on developing her self-confidence, but also her mental toughness. She knew how helpful this would become when she became a business owner in the future. Mental toughness would help Amirah reach her goals just like self-confidence and self-discipline.

Through a series of strategies, Amirah focused on gaining control of her emotions. She started focusing on the comments from her professors about her papers as ways to improve her abilities. She took any type of criticism to develop her mindset. Amirah noticed which friends supported her and who wanted her to party with them. Because partying wouldn't help her mindset, Amirah stopped hanging out with her party friends and focused on her more studious friends.

At her college graduation, Amirah thought about the person she was when she entered college. She remembered being a scared young girl who didn't believe she would finish college. She thought she would drop out because it would become too hard. Now, she is valedictorian and giving her speech in front of thousands of people about mental toughness and how it helps on the road to success. Amirah is now confident that she will one day run a successful business.

Once you reach a stage of mental toughness, you are more satisfied with your life. You feel proud of yourself and what you have accomplished. You understand that failure will happen, but this doesn't mean you can't continue to develop your skills. You don't have to let failure take you off your path. Instead, you will fall forward, pick yourself up, dust yourself off, and try again. You will continue to try until you succeed because your mindset tells you that failure doesn't mean giving up. It means that you are trying, and you will become successful as you continue to work at it.

Part 2: Practice

"We can be truly successful only at something we're willing to fail at."

- Mark Manson

Chapter 4: Think Big, Start Small

You have a list of tasks you want to accomplish. However, it seems that your list of goals continues to grow without you marking any of them off. You start to wonder if you will ever reach some of the goals you set for yourself. As you think about some of your goals, you realize how big they are, but you know you can achieve them—you are not always sure how, but you know it is possible.

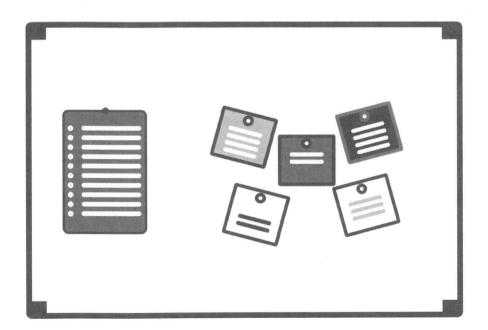

One of the biggest practices when maintaining self-discipline is to create smaller steps for your goals. It doesn't matter how small you think your goal is, you always want to break it down into smaller steps. Think of your goal as the top of your stairs and each step you take is reaching one of the smaller goals that will lead you to achieve your main goal.

You don't want to make the mistake of setting your goal and finding yourself struggling to reach it because you didn't understand how to get started, what to do, or that the goal is too big for you. When you find yourself struggling with your goals, you are more likely to believe that you can't reach them. This will affect you psychologically and damage some of the self-discipline you have built.

Golden Goal Setting Rules

To help you get into the mindset of developing smaller goals within a larger goal, it is important to understand the golden rules when it comes to setting goals.

Write Down Your Goals

How often have you written down your goals, compared to keeping them locked away in your mind? You probably discuss your goals with family, friends, co-workers and other people in your life, but have you ever sat down and written out your goals? If not, physically writing out your goals can help make your goal real to you. While you might feel you want to achieve your goal when you think about it, you have thousands of thoughts going through your mind a day. You might have an idea of how to reach your goal, but how much work you put toward your goal every day? Have you ever forgotten about any goals you want to accomplish or pushed them to the side because you didn't feel they were important enough or you were too busy to focus on them? If so, the real reason you might have forgotten or pushed them away is because you didn't write them down.

When you write your goals down on paper, you want to use words like "will" instead of "might." You want to make the goal as concrete as possible. For example, instead of writing, "I would like to exercise for 30 minutes each day" you write, "I will exercise for 30 minutes every morning."

When you write down your goals, you want to frame them positively. You will write the way you think about your goal, so if you aren't completely sure you will reach your goal this will come out in your writing. Then, when you look at your written goals, you won't feel as strongly about achieving them, especially if you place doubt in your goals. For example, you write, "I will try to stick to my diet and say goodbye to all the yummy food," it isn't a motivational goal. You can feel negatively about this goal because it will make you feel that you are saying goodbye to your favorite foods and forcing yourself on this diet. You want to word the goal in a way that highlights your new diet positively. For example, you write, "I will stick to my diet to improve my overall health."

Use the SMART Rule

You can create goals or SMART goals. SMART stands for the five characteristics that every goal should be expressed as:

- *Specific*. Specific goals are well-defined and clear. You know exactly what you want and what steps you will take to reach your goal.
- *Measurable*. You want to include a plan to measure the progress of your goal. For example, you will have dates that give you a timeline of your goal. If you want to exercise for 30 minutes every morning, you will start by exercising 10 minutes every morning for two weeks. You

will then increase your time by 5 minutes once a week until you reach 30 minutes.

- *Attainable.* Always know that you can achieve the goals you set. Of course, they can seem overwhelming at first, but your confidence will make you believe you can reach your goals. At the same time, you have to ensure that you need to work hard to achieve your goals. If you set goals that are too easy, you won't feel accomplished or grow out of your comfort zone.
- *Relevant.* Make sure your goals are relevant to the direction you want to take in your life. This will help you stay focused on your life's path and reach where you see yourself in three or five years.
- *Time-Bound.* Always make sure your goals have a deadline. The deadline might be in a month or three years. It all depends on the goal and its steps.

Your Goals Need to Keep You Motivated

If you set goals that don't motivate you to work on them, your goal setting won't work. You need to ensure that your goals are important to you and direct you where you want to go in life. If you don't imagine the outcome of your goals or have little interest in them, you need to look at why. Are you thinking about your goal in the right way? Are your goals something that you want to gain in your life? Is your goal a priority?

You need to have the "I must accomplish this goal" attitude to maximize the likelihood of achieving your goals. The result of not following this rule will leave you frustrated and disappointed in yourself.

Goal Setting

S   Specific

M   Measurable

A   Attainable

R   Relevant

T   Time-bound

Creating an Action Plan

Creating an action plan for each goal will help you follow through with them. You will remain excited and each step you accomplish will give you more motivation to achieve your goal. It's not easy to look at a goal and then think about your action plan. To help you get more comfortable with this process, here are some tips to incorporate as you create your plan.

1. Make sure your goals are clear and you know exactly what you want. Think about how you will describe your goal. Ensure that your goal is relevant to your life plans and attainable.

2. Create the steps to reach your goal by going backward. For example, if you want to eliminate your debt within a year, you will look at how much you need to pay off every month, every three months, and during the sixth month period. Having an amount for each of these milestones will help you keep better track of the steps of your goal. Make sure you include a timeframe for each step.

3. Take each step one by one and focus on it. You need to determine what actions are required for you to reach your goal. For example, you will create a budget and

notice where you can save money or what money you can put toward your debt every month.

4. Ask yourself what reward you want to give yourself once you achieve each step and reach your goal. This reward needs to be something that will keep you motivated and something you don't give yourself regularly.

5. Create a daily plan. Ask yourself what you can do every day to make sure you reach your milestones and goals? For example, if you purchase a lunch at work every day, how much money will you save if you pack a lunch from home? Will meal planning help you stick to the schedule? What other daily habits do you have that can help you save money or put it toward your debt?

6. It is common to feel like you have a chaotic paper full of goals and scribbles when you are done creating your plan. If you need to re-write your plan it is best that you do. You want your plan to look clear and easy to follow as this will keep you motivated.

7. Make sure that you remain consistent in your daily schedule. This will help you achieve your milestones. Follow through with the tasks that you give yourself

and remember to stay away from your rewards until you complete a step.

The biggest key when it comes to reaching your goals is to focus on one milestone at the time. Even when you look at your whole goal on the sheet, you want to keep your mind focused on the milestone you are working on at that moment. This will help keep you focused, and you won't feel so overwhelmed by your goal.

When Roger wrote his action plan to help him follow a schedule, he decided to observe his natural behavior for a week and note anything that helped him follow through with his schedule and anything that kept him away from his schedule. The helpful behavior and actions that Roger wrote down included:

- Getting up by 7:00 A.M. and getting dressed.
- Having a healthy breakfast.
- Sitting at my desk by 8:00 A.M.
- Switching my phone on silent and keeping it in another room.
- Keeping the television in my office area/bedroom off.
- Taking a 10-minute break to walk around the apartment every hour, but not turning on the television or sitting down.

- Taking a one-hour lunch break where I leave my work and focus on a relaxing activity.
- Stop working at 6:00 P.M. and relaxing or focusing on other activities the rest of the night instead of continuing to work late or going back to work after an hour.

The behaviors and actions Roger noticed that didn't help him stick to his schedule included:

- Staying up late and allowing myself to sleep in.
- Staying up too late and napping during the day.
- Eating a heavy and unhealthy breakfast.
- Not getting ready for the day, such as starting work while still wearing pajamas.
- Keeping my phone next to me.
- Keeping the silent mode off.
- Having non-work tabs open online.
- Turning on the television or watching a YouTube video when I am on a break.
- Not leaving my desk during my break.
- Working from the time I get up until I go to bed. This decreases my willpower to work the next day.
- Snacking often.
- Taking more than my needed breaks.
- Not standing up to the point when I feel the need to move.

- Telling myself that "I can work on it later in the day. I have time."

Once Roger had a clear understanding of what behaviors and actions helped him and which ones didn't, he started to create his plan. His goal became "I will follow my work schedule of starting at 8:00 A.M. and working until 6:00 P.M. with one 10-minute break every hour and a one-hour lunch break."

Roger then started to write out the steps of his goal. He gave himself a month to accomplish the goal and felt this was an adequate amount of time. The steps Roger included to help him make his goal were:

1. Start going to bed at 11:00 P.M and set an alarm to get up at 7:00 A.M

2. Get up and get ready for the day, just as I would when working outside of my home.

3. Have a healthy breakfast, such as fruit and eggs with a slice of bacon or a sausage patty.

4. Sit at my desk at 8:00 A.M.

5. Work until 8:55, when I will take a break until 9:05. Repeat this break every hour.

6. Take lunch at 11:55 A.M and be back to work at 12:55 P.M.

7. Stop working at 6:00 P.M.

Roger focused on giving himself a few days and worked on one step at a time. Once he went to the next step, he rewarded himself with his favorite ice cream treat. When he reached his goal of keeping to his daily schedule for a week ahead of his deadline, he allowed himself to take a vacation day. Roger continues to follow this schedule and he has found working from home to be more enjoyable as he separates his workday from his personal time with the schedule.

Chapter 5: Yesterday You Said Tomorrow

Scarlett O'Hara from *Gone with the Wind* became famous for saying, "I'll think about that tomorrow" when she came across something that she felt was too difficult or didn't want to think about it when she should (Rice, 2006). While this is often known to bring comic relief into the film, it shows O'Hara's tendency to procrastinate over situations that she should have taken care of at that moment.

Procrastination is when you take extra time to start something or don't focus on a task you should for several reasons. Everyone procrastinates at some point in their life and you probably remember several instances when you have procrastinated. For example, you waited until the last minute to start a paper in high school or college, you didn't finish the assigned reading for class, you decided to put off filling your gas tank until the next morning, or you didn't place your dishes in the dishwasher last night because you didn't feel like it.

Procrastination doesn't always cause more problems within our life. For instance, you can do the dishes or fill up your gas tank the following morning, but you might end up running late for work. There are times where procrastination can cause major problems within our life, especially when it comes to not making a deadline at work.

When you let procrastination get out of hand, it can start to harm you emotionally and psychologically. For example, you had three weeks to work on your presentation for work and now you have two days left. As you look at all the work you have to do to put your presentation together, you start to mentally scold yourself for waiting so long. You tell yourself that you were stupid for procrastinating and you had told yourself last time that you wouldn't allow yourself to do this again. You ask yourself why you can't learn from your previous procrastination mistakes. If you didn't make a deadline at work and need to ask for an extension, you deal with anxiety and worry that you will lose your job because you ask for extensions so often due to your procrastination. You ask yourself, "What is wrong with me? Why can't I just get it and do the work like I should? Why don't I know better?"

Procrastination is one of the main roadblocks you have in your life that keep you from making the right decision and reaching your goals. It can keep you from doing what you want, giving you feelings of regret. It can make you feel like you have opportunities slipping away through your fingertips. You don't feel like you are doing anything meaningful and wasting your time. Procrastination is frustrating and causes people to become so angry with themselves that it affects their mindset.

One of the first steps to understanding your procrastination is to know why you procrastinate. This can change from situation to situation. For example, you struggle with anxiety and have to call your bank because you never received a copy of your title once you finished paying off your loan. While you know it isn't your fault, you think of what your previous loan advisor will say. You worry about becoming embarrassed or what will happen if they can't help you. Instead of contacting the bank the day you needed to, you wait another week, always coming up with excuses for why you can't call them day after day. Another reason you find yourself procrastinating is because you don't like the task. You know you need to clean your home, but you are into a show on Netflix, so you continue to watch the show instead of clean. At the end of the day, you look around your home and become frustrated with yourself because you didn't clean like you said you would that day.

To understand why you procrastinate, you need to assess the situation. Procrastination has a lot to do with your psyche and mindset while other factors focus more on your personality and environment.

- **You saw your role models procrastinate.** For example, if you struggle with cleaning or making deadlines, ask yourself if you noticed this behavior from your parents, grandparents, or other role models growing up. Try to come up with examples so you understand where and when you learned to procrastinate.

- **You lack self-confidence.** Self-confidence has a lot to do with procrastination. For example, if you need to write a story for your creative writing class, but don't believe that you are a good writer you will find yourself putting this assignment off as long as possible.

- **You are a perfectionist.** You might not be a perfectionist when it comes to everything, but when it comes to the task you are procrastinating, you feel that it has to be perfect. You continue to put off the task because you don't know how to make it perfect or you are afraid you can't make it perfect.

- **You struggle with mental illness.** Mental illness affects several parts of your life. For example, if you have anxiety you might become anxious when needing to start a new project. Depression will cause procrastination because you are not interested in the project. Mental illness diminishes your concentration and motivation.

- **You can't focus because you aren't comfortable in your environment.** Are you trying to focus on the task, but find yourself looking around your environment and thinking about how it isn't comfortable? For example, you don't feel it is clean enough or it feels cramped.

- **You feel scared.** If you need to perform a new task, you might procrastinate because you are scared about how you will do. For example, you received a promotion at work. You know that you are a good fit and you are confident in your abilities, but you are scared about what your co-workers and supervisors will think about your work.

Remove Temptations

Roger works from home and he is trying to focus on writing a book for one of his clients. The due date is fast approaching and Roger is afraid he won't make the deadline. While he is working diligently on the project, the topic is more difficult than his other topics. He also finds himself distracted every time he hears his phone. He feels like he has to answer his phone, even when it is a message on his personal social media accounts.

Roger has tried to ignore his phone by putting his ringer and notifications on silent, but he found himself checking his phone every five minutes as he worried, he would miss an important message from a client. Roger tried to place his work app on a different notification sound and only pay attention to this notification tone during work hours, but he still found himself checking his phone. He even tried to leave his phone in a separate room to use the "out of sight, out of mind" concept, but he found himself checking his phone every 15 minutes.

As a way to try to remove the temptation of checking his phone, Roger downloaded his work app onto his computer. He then shut off his phone and placed it in another room. At first, Roger found himself thinking about checking his phone and walking up to turn his phone on every half hour. However, after a couple of days, Roger started to become used to having his phone off and away from him while he was working. He went from checking his phone every half hour to once an hour. Soon, he was only checking his phone during his breaks.

Like most of us, Roger struggled with removing temptations that kept him from working. Temptations are one of the main reasons for procrastination, and it is difficult to remove the temptations as this involves strong self-discipline.

Breaking free of your temptations is sometimes the hardest part about overcoming procrastination and developing your self-discipline. Temptations can be like food cravings for your brain—you need to have it. Because of this, you can treat the temptations that cause you to procrastinate like a craving. For example, you can limit your access. This is what Roger did when he turned his phone off and placed it in another room. Doing this made him think twice about whether he really needed to stop working, get up, walk to his cell phone, turn it on, and wait so he could check it. If your temptation is watching television when you should be working, then you can place your remotes somewhere, so it is more difficult to turn on the television. You can also work in an area where there is no television.

Another way to break free of your temptations is to use the 15 minutes rule. You commit to not allowing yourself to give in to your temptation for 15 minutes. The method to this rule is by the time 15 minutes have passed, your brain is no longer focused on your temptation and you continue to work on your project instead.

Learn to Say No

One of the most difficult words to say for many people is "no." You often feel bad for telling someone that you can't help them with a task or that you feel you need a reason to say no. First, you never need a reason to say 'no' as this word is a sentence all by itself. Second, you should never feel bad about putting yourself first and knowing what you can and cannot handle.

When it comes to your temptation, saying no is different because you aren't telling another person no unless they are asking you to go to the movies with them instead of focusing on your task. You are most likely telling yourself no when it comes to your temptations. This should be easier right? No. In fact, it can be harder to say no to your temptations than to another person.

One of the ways to tell yourself no is by focusing on the difference between "I won't" and "I can't." The difference is your mindset when it comes to the two phrases. When you say "I won't" it implies that you choose not to do something. When you say "I can't" it makes you feel like there is another force stopping you from making the decision and this can cause you to give in to your temptation more. In other words, saying "I won't" gives you more power over the situation.

For example, you are increasing the amount of time you exercise every day. You are finding yourself saying "I can't go another 10 minutes because I am too sore and tired." Instead of saying this, tell yourself, "I am not the type of person to end their workout early" meaning you won't end your workout early. If you find yourself sleeping in late in the morning, tell yourself that you are not the type of person to sleep in as you know it's a waste of time.

Plan of Action

There are many strategies you can follow when creating a plan of action to overcome your temptations. You might feel inspired by the strategies you read here or create your own. If you are stuck when it comes to creating a plan of action, you can focus on these steps as inspiration.

1. **Set a date.** It is important that you set a date to focus on avoiding your temptation. Setting a date helps you prepare for the change in your routine or prepares your mind to know that you will focus on avoiding your temptation starting at a certain time. When you set a time, you will become more successful in your efforts.

2. **Write down the reasons why.** You are more likely to resist your temptation if you understand why you want to avoid it. For example, Roger decided to avoid his phone because it was causing him to fall behind in his work. He wasn't focusing as well when he was writing because he was always mindful of when his phone gave a tone.

3. **Visualize your end result.** Imagine yourself succeeding in avoiding your temptation. For example, Roger imagined that he improved his workflow and didn't need to worry about asking for extensions for his deadlines because he could concentrate on his work instead of his phone.

4. **What to do when your temptation increases?** There are some temptations that you can't completely remove from your environment. When this happens, you need to have a plan in place on what you will do if your temptation

increases and you think about giving in. For example, you can find something different to do. If you feel that you are thinking about your temptation because you need a break from your task, take a break but do something different. Roger is trying to stay away from Netflix during the day because he can't watch just one episode of his favorite television show. This causes him to fall behind on his work. Therefore, when he needs a break, he decides to go for a short walk or read his book instead of watching Netflix.

Create the Right Environment

Creating the right environment means looking all around you to see what is keeping you from achieving your goals and focusing on your tasks. For example, if you work from home, it is best to create an office area where you work. Even if you have a laptop, do your best to work in one spot as this will condition your mind to know that when you sit at your desk, it is time to work.

You also want to look beyond your office and home walls and notice who you hang out with and call your friends. Are they helping you achieve your goals, or do they slow you down? If people don't support you, then it is time to let them go. You want to distance yourself from them as much as possible. It is important that you have people in your life who support your goals and dreams as this will help you become more successful.

It isn't easy to let people go who don't have your best interest at heart. It is important to remember that you don't have to end the relationship completely — and you always need to be honest with them. First, try to communicate with the person. Tell them what you have noticed as they might not understand your goals or their actions. They might try to focus more on supporting you. However, if you don't notice a change in their behavior, you need to limit contact with them.

Strategies to Help You Overcome Procrastination

We discussed removing temptations and creating the right environment separately as those are the two biggest strategies to help you overcome procrastination. There are many other strategies that people use we will discuss in this section.

It is important to note that you can use any strategy you are comfortable with. You might find yourself using more than one strategy and you might find that you only need one strategy at the time. What you choose is directly up to you. You need to make sure that you are comfortable with it, yet you need to keep yourself a little uncomfortable so you can continue to achieve your goals.

Find a Mentor

You want to seek out someone who already overcame their struggles with procrastination. They can help you through the process and be a sense of support that will allow you to feel that you can achieve your goal, especially when you find yourself struggling to do so. There will always be days where you feel that your steps and goal process is easier than other days. During the difficult days, you will need someone, or several people, on your side to give you support to keep going. Your mentor will be the main person and never let you give up. They will work with you through any struggles that you have and help you reevaluate your goals if needed.

Don't Overcomplicate Anything

It is easy to overthink and make situations more complicated than they are, especially when you are trying to reach goals. You might feel that you can't start on a certain day because it is not the right time. You might continue to push your goal back because you don't feel that you have the right mindset to start focusing on your goals. All of the problems and excuses you use to justify putting off your goal makes everything more complicated. For example, Roger wanted to focus on his goal of getting up at 6:00 A.M. for months as this allowed him two hours to relax in the morning before work. The problem was that Roger would continue to relax in bed and kept telling himself he would hit "snooze" as this was relaxing. Suddenly, Roger would notice it was 7:30 A.M and he was about to be late for work.

Once Roger started working from home, he continued to hit snooze until almost 8:00 A.M. or later because he made his own hours. This caused problems because Roger had less energy to focus on work when he slept in so late. He would find himself working slowly or becoming easily distracted until 1:00 in the afternoon. It was at this time he would start to kick himself for not working earlier on his project. Roger's emotions toward himself created more complications for his mindset, which made him struggle to stick to his schedule more.

You might over-complicate matters when you feel that the situation needs to be perfect. Not only do you need to start at a certain time, but you have to know a certain amount of information, your office area needs to be perfect, and you need to work without making any mistakes. When this happens, you allow your perfectionism to take control. You always need to remember that nothing is perfect. You do the best job you can do, learn from your mistakes, and move on. Once you realize what you can control and what you can't, you start to focus on what you can control, and situations become less complicated. This also helps with your mindset as you are less likely to become frustrated with your mistakes.

Break Your Work into Small Steps

The struggle people have when it comes to their goals is looking at it as one big picture, which is why it is important to break your goals into smaller steps. You want to take the same action when you are focusing on your work that you feel is too daunting, even if it is your whole workday.

Roger knew that starting his own writing and editing business and working from home meant that he wouldn't have a typical 9 to 5 office type job. Some days he would work 12 or more hours and other days he would work eight or less. Roger also understood that there could be times he worked during the weekend and didn't take a day off for weeks. He was prepared to take on this schedule. However, once he started working from home, he began to feel overwhelmed and found himself procrastinating worse than ever.

Other than creating a schedule and limiting his distractions, Roger's mentor told him to break his workday down into smaller steps just as he does his goals. At first, Roger wasn't sure how to go about this task. He couldn't comprehend how to break down his workday as he would just be writing and editing throughout the day. This is when his mentor stepped in to help him. First, Roger needed to write down everything he does in one day.

He wrote:

- Check email and direct messages.
- Research
- Write
- Edit
- Look for other work once a project is complete

To help Roger come up with a more complete list, his mentor asked him how he manages his projects. Roger says he only allows himself to have four to five projects at a time because he knows he can work for an hour and a half to two hours on each project every day. Therefore, Roger's mentor told him to include each project into his phases. Roger created a new list that looked like the following:

- Check email and direct messages
- Work on project one from 8:00 to 10:30 A.M.
- Work on project two from 10:30 A.M. to 11:55 A.M.
- Work on project three from 12:55 A.M. to 2:30 P.M.
- Work on project four from 2:30 P.M. to 4:00 P.M.
- If I have a project five, work on that from 4:00 P.M. to 5:30 P.M.
- If I don't have a fifth project, work on the project that is due first.
- Finish up the day between 5:30 to 6:00 P.M.

Once Roger's day was broken down into steps, he could focus on one step at a time. This helped Roger feel more comfortable about managing his projects and gave him more motivation to complete his tasks. Roger found that when he worked on one project at a time, he became bored with the project. He would become more distracted in the afternoon as he felt he needed a break from the project, but he knew he had to continue. If he took a break, he usually took a long break because it was hard for him to get motivated to sit back at his desk. By working on four to five projects in a day, Roger knows he is making progress on each project every day and he doesn't become distracted easily.

Chapter 6: Increase Your Self-Confidence

"With realization of one's own potential and self-confidence in one's ability, one can build a better world."

– Dalai Lama

We have already discussed what self-confidence is, so now it is time to look at how you can improve your self-confidence through a variety of strategies. One factor to remember is that as you are working on your self-discipline, even if it is only in one area in your life, you are naturally improving your self-confidence. Once you build your self-confidence in one area in your life, you will start to feel more confident in other areas of your life.

When Roger started writing, he didn't have a lot of self-confidence in his abilities. He felt that he was a good writer, but he didn't believe his writing would take him anywhere. He didn't believe that he could support himself and his family with a writing career, even though this is what he wanted to do. Roger had always loved writing, ever since he was a young child, but he didn't have a lot of people tell him that he was good at writing. In fact, his parents told him that he couldn't go anywhere with his writing and that he should decide on another career.

The first job Roger received as a freelance writer was for a small article about Thanksgiving. His client loved the article, but never got in touch with him to write another article. Roger received jobs from online blogs, but most were on a volunteer basis. About nine months into his freelance career, Roger thought about giving up and sticking with his office job. However, he received a position as a writer for a ghostwriting company. Roger wasn't positive that he could give them the high-quality writing they wanted, but he decided to give it a try.

Within two months, Roger became one of the company's top writers. His supervisors praised his work and told him that he was an amazing writer. He received great reviews from the editors, but still struggled to believe that he was a good writer. As Roger continued to develop as a writer, he continued to improve his writing. At the same time, his self-confidence as a writer improved. Within six months on the job, Roger left his employer and created his own writing company. He started writing full-time at home and knew he would continue to improve as a writer. Roger started to believe what his editors and supervisors told him about his writing, which improved his self-confidence on the job.

Over time, Roger noted that his self-confidence also improved in his personal life. He believed that he could learn new tasks. He started to focus on hobbies that he previously didn't believe he could accomplish. He began to hold conversations with people he barely knew and confidently told them his opinions and thoughts, even if the other people didn't agree with him. Because of the confidence, Roger gained from his job as a writer, he gained confidence in other areas of his life.

How to Build Your Self-Confidence

It is important to note that no one has a limit when it comes to self-confidence. You are not born with only 10% of self-confidence or the ability to grow your self-confidence to 25%. People who exhibit strong self-confidence have worked on building their confidence for years. Even if they grew up in a loving home with supportive and encouraging parents, they still worked on building their self-confidence when they left home. Self-confidence is a part of your mindset that you will constantly develop.

There is no right or wrong limit when it comes to self-confidence. Some people are afraid to act confident about their abilities because they worry, they will seem narcissistic or arrogant to someone. Someone with strong self-confidence is not narcissistic. Narcissism is a personality disorder that causes people to believe they are the best at everything. They believe there is no one better than them and they will do anything in their power to remain on top — even hurting other people. Self-confidence shines in people and makes them more likely to help other people. They want to see other people succeed, just as they have succeeded. They work hard and understand that they will continue to improve their skills. They know they can learn from other people and are willing to do what they can to ensure they help themselves and others.

There are many strategies you can use when you work on building your self-confidence. You might find yourself starting with one strategy and once you have more self-confidence, looking into a new strategy. This happens because as your self-confidence grows, your methods will also develop. You will start to focus on other areas of your life, or you will start to notice you need to build on certain personality traits and this takes different strategies. No matter where you sit with your self-confidence, here are a few strategies that you can incorporate into your life.

Use Affirmations

One of the biggest ways people start to increase their self-confidence is through affirmations. These are uplifting and positive sayings that you can read wherever you are, through books or by Googling positive or motivational quotes. When you are using affirmations to build your self-confidence, you want to focus on quotes that will lift your spirits. For example, if you are struggling when it comes to your job, you can look at quotes that are more specific in your field of study or quotes that focus on any career.

You always want to say the affirmation out loud. You can read it in your mind first, but you will believe the message more if you read it out loud.

Take a moment to say the following quote in your head:

"The best way to predict the future is to create it."

- Abraham Lincoln

Now, take time to reflect on how that quote made you feel. Did you think much about it or did you read it like you read anything else? People often read quotes in their mind like they will read a novel. While they can feel the quote bringing them a sense of peace or creating more positivity, it doesn't last long. In fact, it only lasts a matter of seconds for most people. Now, take a moment to say the following quote out loud:

"The most important thing is to look ahead. The past is your anchor."

- Maxime Lagace

Once again, reflect on what you read out loud. Did you notice any difference from when you read Abraham Lincoln's quote in your head? Did you find yourself thinking about Maxime Lagace's quote more than Lincoln's quote? Most people will notice that they not only take the quote more seriously when they read it out loud, but it sticks in their mind longer. They focus more on the meaning of the quote and how it relates to them.

Another trick to affirmations is to remain consistent. The more often you speak a quote, the more you will believe what you are reading. You don't need to read the same quote over and over again. You can always read a new quote, but it should be positive. The more positive quotes you read throughout your day, the stronger your self-confidence will become. Because you start to feel more positive mentally, you will start to become more positive emotionally. Your mental and emotional positivity will radiate into physical positivity, making you feel better overall.

You don't have to read other people's positive quotes to get yourself to focus on affirmations. You can focus on your own affirmations by looking at the areas in your life where you want to build your confidence. The key is to say them in a way that is a question. This is because your brain naturally wants to seek out answers to questions. For example, during her college years, Amirah noticed professors praised her written papers and essay questions. They told her she was an excellent writer, which is something Amirah had never thought about before. In fact, she never wanted to become a writer. But she knew that she needed to use this as a tool to help build her mental toughness and mindset. So, she asked herself, "Why am I a good writer?" instead of telling herself, "I am a good writer."

Take a moment to think about an area where you want to improve your self-confidence. This could be at your job, school, or your mindset. Then, tell yourself what you are good at by saying, "I am good at ____." Now, it is time to turn that statement into a question. Ask yourself, "Why am I good at ____." Reflect on how you continue to think about this question as your brain is trying to find an answer. You might come up with a few reasons why you are good at the task within a few minutes or might find yourself continuing to think about the question throughout the day. Take time at the end of your day to reflect on the exercise.

Imagine What You Want to Become

Since you were younger, you wanted to become someone. You might remember who you wanted to become in kindergarten, such as a teacher, firefighter, police officer, or an animal. Children have wild imaginations but believe that anything they imagine is possible. The main reason for this is because they visualize themselves as what they want to be. For example, if you wanted to be a firefighter you imagined yourself fighting a house fire and becoming a hero. As a teacher, you imagined teaching a class and enjoying your time with your students.

Unfortunately, using the visualization technique is something that people push off to the side like a child's play. Older children, teenagers, and adults shouldn't visualize like children because people are meant to outgrow this stage, right? Wrong. This is one of the biggest myths when it comes to self-confidence. The truth is, the more you visualize who you want to become, the stronger your confidence grows in that area. Of course, confidence is a snowball effect, which means that once it begins to develop in one area, it will develop in other areas. You might not notice this development, but one day you will reflect on where you were a year ago and where you are now and notice your growth, which will astound you.

Sometimes people need help with visualization, and this is fine. There is nothing wrong with creating a visualization board that shows pictures of your goals and where you see yourself within a year. Creating a vision board is easy and cheap. You can cut pictures from magazines and glue them onto a cardboard backing or print off pictures that relate to your goals and glue them. You can also draw pictures, use quotes, or specific words that help you stay focused on your goals.

You want to place your vision board somewhere in your home so you will see it every day. It is important that you spend time reflecting on your vision board in the morning or before you go to bed for at least 10 minutes every day. Look carefully at the pictures and think about your progress with each image.

Many people like to include journaling with their vision boards. As they are reflecting, they will discuss the steps they completed that day to help them reach their goals. Journaling is beneficial because it allows you to think about what you have accomplished. For example, if you are having a tough day and feel that your self-confidence is a little lower than normal, you can look through your journal and notice all the improvements you have made over a certain period of time.

Help Someone Else

Many people focus on building their self-confidence by helping someone else. This person can be a friend, family member, or stranger. You might find yourself volunteering at a local nonprofit, such as a food pantry or setting up a drive for people who are in the middle of a natural disaster. You might decide you will help one person every day and make this part of your routine. No matter what you decide to do, helping someone else is a guaranteed way to build up your self-confidence because it makes you feel good.

Take a moment to think about a time when you helped someone. No matter who the person is, remember how you felt after you knew you helped them. If you need to, take time to remind yourself of the situation and then allow your feelings to come to you naturally. As you think about the moment, your emotions will start to come to the surface.

One of the reasons helping someone helps us build our self-confidence is because we forget about ourselves for a moment. We don't think about our troubles. Instead, we become more grateful for what we have in life. We start to see our lives in a different way. This means, the more you help someone, the stronger your self-confidence will become as you will continue to feel blessed in your life.

For example, you tend to focus on your weaknesses and believe that you can't become the person you want to become. You are working on becoming your best self, a person who believes they will succeed, can save money, works hard, doesn't procrastinate and can control their emotions. However, you find yourself struggling to reach even a part of the person you want to become. This all starts to change when you walk into your church one Sunday and see a group of women sewing. You ask them what they are doing, and they tell you that they are knitting and sewing scarves, hats, and gloves to ship to people all over the world so they can stay warm during the winter. You then ask how you can become a part of this process and they tell you to join them anytime.

Even though you don't know anything about sewing or knitting, they take the time to help you. Soon, you are a part of a group that is shipping six boxes filled with winter items to children in Alaska. You smile as you see the boxes leave the church and the UPS truck drive off. As you think about this process, you realize how much you believe in yourself because you are helping children stay warm during the winter months.

Do One Thing that Scares You Every Day

Like most people, you want to stay away from the factors that scare you. You don't want to face fears because it is uncomfortable, and you never know what will happen. For example, if you want to go to a haunted house tour for Halloween, but you are scared about the setup from people dressed as Zombies to people jumping out, you are more than likely going to stay away from haunted houses. You might worry about screaming when someone jumps out at you and people will think that you are stupid or too scared to handle a situation like this. Even though you want to go with your friends to a haunted house every Halloween, you come up with a reason for why you can't every year. Other risks that might scare you include getting started on your own business, picking up a new hobby, or cleaning out your storage closet because you haven't been there for years.

As you plan your day, you want to think about one thing that scares you. This could be something that makes you feel uncomfortable, something that gives you anxiety when you think about it, or something that makes you want to run and hide. As you focus on your morning routine, write down the one item you will do that day that you are afraid of. Doing something every day that puts a little fear in you helps you become comfortable with being uncomfortable. It builds your confidence because you start to realize your potential. Instead of telling yourself, "I can't do that" or "That sounds a bit scary" you tell yourself, "I did it."

Set Yourself Up to Win

Not only do you want to focus on setting up for your goal, but you also want to make sure you set yourself up to win. This means you don't want to make your goals or steps hard to achieve. You want to make them easy, yet you don't want them to be too easy. At the same time, it is important to remember that when you are trying to overcome a challenge, steps might look too easy when you write them down on paper. For example, setting a goal to get up at 7:00 in the morning can seem easy and not challenging at all. However, when you are in the habit of sleeping in until 8:00 A.M. or don't get up to an alarm, the step is a little harder, especially if you don't have strong self-discipline to get up when your alarm goes off. People can hit snooze several times or turn their alarm off and then easily fall back asleep. You want to avoid this when you are setting your goals and trying to stick to them.

Another way to set yourself up to win is to make your first two steps easier than your other steps. For example, you can increase the difficulty of each step of your goal. This will help you get a start with your goals and then keep you motivated and give you a little extra challenge with each step. This can help you overcome any discomfort you have with your goal or become a part of doing one thing that scares you. It is always possible to combine two strategies at the same time.

When You are Struggling, Look at What You Have Already Achieved

Everyone has moments when they become frustrated with their goals and you are no different. You might feel that you can't reach your goal because you continue to make a mistake during one step, or you don't think to feel that you set your goal too high. You might have a bad day and don't have any energy to focus on your goals, even if it is a part of your daily routine. Roger finds himself struggling when one of his clients request a revision. Even though the clients ask Roger to switch a few things around and tell him they loved his writing and appreciate how much work he put into the book, he still feels like he made a mistake and disappointed his client with the revision. Roger understands that his clients are excited to receive their finished product and want to send it to publication as soon as they receive it. He knows having to wait for revisions can set them back a few days.

Roger used to find himself taking revisions so hard that it became difficult for him to focus on his work for the rest of the day. There were times that he felt he couldn't focus on his work the next day because he kept thinking about the revision he needed to do. This caused Roger to fall behind on his goal setting, which mentally and emotionally made matters worse for Roger.

To help himself stay out of a downward spiral when he received a revision, Roger talked to his mentor. Roger's mentor told him that revisions are a part of the ghostwriting business. If he received any bad reviews or comments, he should reevaluate his work and see if the client's comments are justified. Roger's mentor stated that while they usually are, you can't please everyone, and you need to be prepared for the client who will never be truly happy with their project. The mentor also told Roger that he should take any other revisions as to what they are. If a client loves the work but wants a few things changed, then you make those changes.

Once Roger told himself that there are revisions when it comes to his business, he became more comfortable when he received a revision. He understood that it was an opportunity for growth and not something he should be ashamed of. Instead of struggling with the revision, Roger would go back and read the positive comments he received from his clients. helped lift his spirits, so he didn't back away from his work. In fact, Roger found that he became more motivated to make the projects even better when he received reviews.

Chapter 7: Build Willpower

When you have strong willpower, you control your impulses. You know what you need to do to reach your goal or get the job done. Willpower is an important part of self-discipline because it helps you focus on what you need to do instead of what you want to do.

Everyone has some type of willpower. You might have the willpower to help you get tasks done when you are close to your deadline. You might find that your willpower is stronger when you first receive your task and get it started than when you are approaching the deadline. While some people can tell themselves "no" easily and follow through with their decision, other people don't have that strong of willpower and find themselves bending to their desires.

Two Main Parts of Building Willpower

There are two main parts when it comes to building willpower. The first part is motivation and the second part is tracking your progress. Through these two factors, your willpower will slowly build and help you stay on track with your goals.

Before we discuss the two main parts, it is important to take time to discuss consistency. While this has been briefly mentioned before, when you are working on willpower, you need to make sure that you follow through with your plan every time. For example, for every goal you set, you want to have some type of tracking system that shows the progress you have made. By remaining consistent in these efforts, your goal setting and tracking system will become more of a habit than something you need to do. You will want to follow through with the system because you understand the benefits and you know what the outcome will be if you continue to remain consistent.

An example of how important consistency is and what it can do for you is the story of Samantha. As a freshman in college, Samantha struggled to make her classes. She felt that because everyone posted the work online and attendance was not part of her grade, she didn't need to go to class all the time. Instead, she would go to class if she needed to hand in an assignment, talk to her professor because she was having a problem understanding her classwork, or when there was a test or quiz. Samantha also told herself that if she found her grades were lower than a B, she would go to the class until her grades improved and then she could start to miss classes again.

Because Samantha found herself missing so many class periods, she didn't meet a lot of new people. When she did show up to class, she felt out of place and that everyone knew she hadn't been in class lately. She felt that the professor judged her for only coming to class on certain days. She started to believe that no one thought she would graduate from college.

Because Samantha missed so many classes, it quickly became a habit. She soon found herself missing important days, such as a day a quiz was scheduled because she didn't remember when her classes were. Soon, Samantha's habit was to miss classes instead of going to classes. At the end of the semester, Samantha received word that she was on academic probation and would be kicked out of school if she didn't improve her grade point average to 2.5.

After talking to her older sister, Samantha realized that her willpower to go to class diminished because she rarely went. Therefore, she felt it took more energy to go to class than to stay home and complete the assignments online or give her professor an excuse that she wasn't feeling well so she could make up a quiz. Samantha's sister told her that she needs to consistently go to class to build her motivation for her classes.

Once she became more motivated, she would find that she wanted to make it to her classes.

The next semester Samantha made it a goal that she would only miss classes for an emergency or when she was sick. She wrote down in her planner whenever she made the class and when she struggled to find the energy to go to class, Samantha looked back at her planner to see that she hadn't missed class yet. Feeling proud of herself, she continued to go to class. By the fourth week of class, Samantha felt she had to get to class. When she came down with the flu in the sixth week, she felt bad for missing class and struggled to stay home and take care of herself instead of going to class.

For Samantha, remaining consistent in going to class and tracking the days she went to class, kept her motivated to continue the process. At the end of the semester, Samantha found herself on the Dean's List and rarely missed a class during the remainder of her college career.

Motivating Yourself

It is true, it is easy to motivate other people. It is hard to motivate yourself because it is easier to tell yourself, "I can do this later, I will have time," or "I can think about this tomorrow when I feel better and more motivated. Everyone deserves a day off." It is easier to listen to someone when they tell you to remain motivated or go to class because you don't want to disappoint them. You want your parents, friends, siblings, or significant others to be proud of you. Therefore, you tend to listen to their requests over your own.

Motivating yourself is an important part of your daily life. You need to motivate yourself to get up when your alarm goes off. You need to motivate yourself to make supper after a busy day. You need to motivate yourself to work instead of surfing the internet. You probably don't even realize all the times you need to motivate yourself throughout the day.

There are several techniques you can use to help motivate yourself:

1. **Get Positive.** It is easier for other people to motivate you because they are excited and positive. Some people feel silly when they try to make themselves feel excited and positive about a task they need to take on. However, it is essential to help get yourself motivated. The more excited and positive you are about completing the task, the more motivation you will have to focus on the task. Give yourself a pep talk if you need to. You can stand in front of the mirror to do this or talk to yourself out loud.

2. **Surround yourself with people that will pressure you.** Talk to people, such as your friends and family, about your

goals. Ask them if they will be your sense of support when you are working on the task. If they want to see you succeed, they will agree to be your support. Tell them that there will be times they need to pressure you to get the job done or make sure that you are on track with your progress.

3. **Always give yourself rewards.** Once you complete a step or a task, give yourself a reward. The reward is there to keep you motivated so you continue working on the next part of your task or move on to a new goal.

4. **Get started, as the motivation will come.** You might be one of those people who finds motivation once they get a project started. If you like to see a project through to the end, it might be helpful to start the project and then look for your motivation. Chances are, you will find it as now that you have started the project, you need to make sure you finish it.

5. **Get motivated through music.** If you are the type of person that likes to work with background noise, you might find yourself more motivated to work when you have some of your favorite songs playing in the background. It is important to analyze if music will really help you with motivation and what type of music. For example, Amirah can concentrate on a task while listening

to some of her favorite songs while Roger finds himself becoming distracted as he would rather listen to music than work. Therefore, Roger listens to classical or relaxing music that plays softly in the background.

6. **Compare yourself to yourself.** Like most people, you are probably good at comparing yourself to other people. You see your co-workers working hard at their tasks and wonder why you don't have this motivation yourself. You compare yourself to your friends who have more money, a bigger home, and nicer cars. You wonder why you can't get to that point and if it is because you don't work as hard. Instead of comparing yourself to other people, it is time to compare yourself to you. Look at your progress and think about the person you used to be when you first started the job. For example, Roger didn't have the confidence as a writer when he first started that he does now. Because of this confidence, Roger has become a stronger writer. When Roger compares himself, he notices how far he has come and can't help but become more motivated to continue on his path.

Recording Your Progress

There are different ways to track your progress and it is important to focus on a method that works for you. The key is to be consistent with your method as this will keep you motivated to record your progress on a task every day. You can use one of the methods discussed below or you can create your own method. You want to do something that is comfortable and will work with your lifestyle. For example, Roger doesn't have to worry about getting ready for bed or putting kids to bed, so he records his progress after his evening meal. Amirah has a hectic schedule that often takes her away at certain times of the day. She doesn't always know when she will be home and when she won't, so she records her progress right before she goes to bed.

Start at zero but set a daily goal.

This method helps when you are trying to increase your exercise, or you want to walk many miles a day. The key is to always start at zero and try to reach a daily goal. For example, if you have a Fitbit, you have a certain number of steps you want to reach every day. At midnight, your watch starts at zero and records every step you make throughout the day. When you reach your goal, your watch makes a noise or vibrates, letting you know that your goal is met. This is the same idea you want to follow with other goals. For instance, you want to exercise for 30 more minutes every day. You will start at zero and then see how many minutes you exercised by the end of each day. You will record this progress in a journal or through a data tracker.

Journaling.

One of the most common methods of tracking progress is to write in a journal. You don't have to spend a lot of time writing in the journal every day, most people can detail their progress within five minutes. However, it is important that you take the time to write about your progress, even if you are more tired than usual or don't feel like writing that evening. You don't want to put it off until morning because you could forget to write down important tracking information and you get out of your system. You can keep this journal as your tracking journal, but if you are working on more than one goal, you want to make sure you separate your goals into different sections. You don't want to write about different goals on the same page as this can become confusing when you look back at your progress.

Excel spreadsheet or Microsoft Word.

Another way you can track your progress is by creating an excel spreadsheet or using Microsoft word. Doing this allows you to create a document that works for your system and keep it updated when you are on your computer. For example, you might find the best time to track your work progress is at the end of your workday.

There are four main steps when it comes to tracking your progress, no matter what method you use:

Look at the bigger picture.

When you go through your day, you often follow the same pattern. This can lead to mindless thoughts and keep you from focusing on what you need to do. When you look at the big picture as you track your goals, you ask yourself a series of questions, such as "What do I want to accomplish?" and "What do I need to do to get my day started?" By thinking about these questions, you will visualize the result you want. This will get you started on focusing on your tasks and help you know what factors you need to consider when you are tracking your progress.

Organize and plan your time.

Get a planner to help you stay on track with your goals. Write down what you want to achieve every day when it comes to your goals. Even if you only want to achieve calling your friends to see if they will become a source of motivation, you want to write this down. After all, part of reaching your goals is having a support network. When you know how long it should take you to reach your milestones, write them in your planner. For example, if you want to get to the second milestone in 10 days, write this down.

Don't do this alone.

You need to find a partner that wants to focus on the same goal or someone that will be your accountability partner. This person can help you stay on track by motivating you to continue and helping you understand your progress. They can look to see where you are with your progress and notice if you are on track or not.

Remember to celebrate your success.

You want to write down your celebrations just as you do your progress.

You Will Feel Drained

You don't want to read that a task you are taking on will make you feel drained. However, it is important that you understand working toward self-development, even when you are focusing on small steps can make you feel overwhelmed. You will have moments where you want to throw in the towel because you don't think you can accomplish your goal. You will have moments when your self-confidence seems low because you start bringing yourself down with your thoughts about how you aren't on track with your goal and you are a failure.

Emotions and mental work drain us and working toward a goal is mental and emotional work. You don't have to have a labor-intensive job to feel tired at the end of a workday. People who have a mentally intensive job can feel just as drained as people with a physically intensive job. It is not a competition and you should never feel that you don't work as hard as someone who works construction.

Another way working toward self-discipline is draining is because you are trying to better yourself. This requires a lot of focus and more work than you are used to. Even though recording your progress might only take five to ten minutes out of your day, you can feel drained when you need to reflect on your day every evening.

It is important that you realize the effort and focus you put toward your self-discipline and all its step is draining, but this should not scare you away. In fact, if it does, this should give you more motivation to focus on developing your self-discipline.

No matter how drained you feel at the end of the day, you have made progress and have increased your self-discipline.

This is one reason why tracking your progress is so important, it helps you stay focused, especially during the tough days where you feel like you aren't making any type of progress.

If you go through a day where you don't focus on any of your progress, it is important that you don't take this to heart. Everyone has days when trying to find motivation is harder than any other task that day. Instead of emotionally and mentally beating yourself up over it, you want to think about it as a mental health day of progress. You needed a break, which everyone does from time to time. Take your mental health day and focus on reenergizing yourself for the next phase in mastering your self-discipline.

You Must Be Willing to Fail

Failing is not easy, especially when you are focused on a task and want to do your best. However, you need to remember that you can't have success without failures. When you fail, this gives you an opportunity to learn and grow. The key when it comes to failures is to fall forward. This means that you will use the opportunity to improve your weaknesses and learn from your mistakes. Even some of the most well-known movie stars received rejections, especially in their early days. Some of them have movies that didn't make it to the big screen while others are open about the failures they have had in their careers. Remember, when you fail, you are not alone in this process as everyone fails at some point within their lives — many times throughout their lives at that.

Chapter 8: Control Your Mind

Becoming the master of your mind takes a lot of willpower, focus, and determination. However, it is essential to master your self-discipline. You always want to remember that the best tool you have to give yourself a better life and reach your best self, is your mind. This means you need to be in control of your thoughts to reach your self-discipline mastery.

The first step you need to take when it comes to taking control of your mind is to know your inner critic. This is the part of you that wants to drag you down and gives you your most unhealthy thoughts. Your inner critic developed throughout your life. It developed from people who told you that you wouldn't succeed, through your parents when they criticized you, through bullies, and from comparing yourself to other people. It is important to remember that your inner critic is you. You are the one who is thinking these negative thoughts and sometimes emotionally and mentally abusing yourself. It is time to face yourself and realize that if you wouldn't treat anyone else this way, why should you treat yourself in this manner. Start to silence your inner critic.

You might have other parts of yourself that you need to learn to let go of before you can truly take control of your mind. For example, if you have anxiety and excessively worry, you need to work on overcoming this worry to gain control of your mind. One of the techniques to help manage anxiety or worry is to think of this piece of you as a little person or monster sitting on your shoulder. You can decorate the little person however you want. For example, you can imagine it looking like an ugly troll. This troll is what whispers those worries and anxieties into your ear which causes you to focus on them instead of what you should be focusing on, which is developing your self-discipline. When you are anxious or worried and hear these thoughts, take control of them by telling your anxiety troll that she is not right. Instead, tell the troll what is true. For instance, if your troll tells you that you will fail your exam, tell her that you won't because you are intelligent, you studied, and you are confident you know the material. As you are telling your troll the truth, imagine it getting smaller and smaller with each word. Eventually, your troll is so small, and its voice is so tiny and squeaky that you don't have any more anxiety about your exam.

Maintaining Focus

Once you have let go of the struggles within yourself, such as anxiety and your inner critic, you can start to work on improving your focus. There are several strategies that you can use to improve your focus. You want to find the best methods for yourself. However, there are many strategies that everyone should follow as they will help you maintain your focus throughout the day.

Start Your Morning with a Routine

There are many ways to start your morning off with a routine. You might find yourself in the kitchen making coffee. Once you have about a half of a cup of coffee, you head to get ready for the day. From there, you decide that you will take 10 minutes to do something that helps you become more focused on your day. For example, you will meditate, read, or exercise. You might try several methods before you settle on one that helps you maintain your focus best throughout the day.

Focus on Good Fats in Your Food

There are tons of diets in the world, but some of the most popular are ones focus on limiting carbohydrates and getting more healthy fats into your body. For example, many people are starting to follow the Ketogenic diet because you eat so many healthy fats throughout your day that your body starts using fats to burn energy instead of carbohydrates. This makes people feel more energized and improves their focus naturally. If you are looking for a diet, as losing weight and eating healthier is one of your goals, you should look into a diet that focuses more on healthy fats than eating smaller portions.

Keep an Hour by Hour Planner

There are several types of planners that you can find in stores. You can get a planner that looks like a wall calendar or one that gives you more room to write down your main tasks during your day. You can also find planners that are broken down into hours. Many people feel the best planner to choose is a motivational planner that will list the hours as this allows you to write down your main task for every hour. For example, Roger takes on four to five projects at once and likes to work on them all throughout his day. Therefore, he found the hourly planner to be the best fit for him because he can write down the project he is working on and even his breaks to help him keep to his schedule.

Get Enough Sleep

Getting enough sleep is often a tip for focusing that is overlooked. Like most people, you have a busy life and it seems that every minute of every day is accounted for. This means that you sometimes find yourself staying up later at night so you can relax by watching a movie. Unfortunately, this cuts down on the amount of sleep you get that night, which can affect you the following day and make it harder for you to maintain your focus. Even if you feel that you should complete a task that night, you want to set a bedtime and stick to it so you can make sure to get at least 7 to 8 hours of good sleep every night.

Meditation

One of the most popular forms of controlling your mind is through meditation. Like most people, once you start meditating, you will quickly find the benefits that allow you to maintain focus, control your mind, control your emotions, and improve your mental and emotional health — which will further improve your physical health.

There are different types of meditation and you can focus on any type. But, because it is helpful to be mindful when you are building your self-discipline, it is best to focus on mindfulness meditation. You want to set aside at least 10 minutes every day for meditation.

Most people focus on this in the morning as meditation helps clear your mind and gets you more motivated for your day. However, this can be tough for some people, especially if there are small children because you need to limit distractions so you can focus well. Many parents find it best to get up about half an hour earlier than the rest of their family so they can take time to meditate.

To incorporate mindful meditation into your life, follow these steps:

1. Find a quiet place where you won't be interrupted. You want to focus on your meditation and not the noise that is

going on inside of your home. Some people like to play meditation music to help drown out any noise around their homes. But you don't want to play the music too loudly as this can distract you when you are trying to meditate.

2. Find a comfortable spot to sit or lay down. The key is to be comfortable so you can focus on your thoughts and not the fact that your leg is falling asleep or you are starting to feel uncomfortable.

3. You want to keep your body straight, but you don't want to become too stiff. Make sure that your spine's natural curvature is there as this will keep you comfortable and focused on the task.

4. Ensure your arms are parallel to your upper body. You can rest your hands on the top of your legs.

5. Some people like to close their eyes while others will keep their eyes open. If you keep your eyes open, don't focus on one object.

6. Start to focus on your breathing. Begin by breathing normally. Notice how your body feels when you inhale and exhale.

7. After you become more relaxed, take a few deep and slow breaths as this will help your body completely relax.

8. Some people like to "follow" their breath. This means the visualize air going in and out of their bodies. Some people take this a bit farther and will imagine any negative energy leaving their body when they exhale and positive energy entering their body when they inhale.

9. At some point, your mind will stop focusing on your breathing and you will start thinking random thoughts. For example, you might think about what you need to do that day, what you need to pick up at the grocery store, how you need to prepare the evening meal, what activities your children have that day, etc.

10. Acknowledge every thought and then let it leave your mind. The key is to start focusing your thoughts.

11. Every minute or so, you should turn your attention back to your breathing as this will keep you from focusing on a thought too long.

12. Once you are done meditating, gently start to bring yourself back into the motions of the room. You can do this by focusing on an item or listening to the noise that is happening inside of your home. You want to bring yourself out of your haze gently, so you don't feel rushed. You want to hold on to that calm feeling as long as possible.

Chapter 9: Change Your Habits

Coming to this point, you might be surprised how the last tips you are receiving have changed from the psychological ones to tips that people haven't been doing before such as the meditation, and to those, you have always known, such as eating, sleeping, exercising. The point to this is because when people start to focus on success, they tend to lose sight of the basics, such as eating and sleeping right. People tend to focus more on what is going to give them the biggest success and less on the fundamentals that will help you maintain a healthy mindset.

It is important that you always follow the four principles of a healthy lifestyle, no matter where you are in your self-discipline mastery. These four principles will help you stay focused on the tasks and give you the best chances of success. The four principles are:

1. **Drinking right.** You want to drink at least two liters of water or eight 8oz glasses every day. While you can drink milk and other fluids throughout your day, water is the most important.

2. **Eating healthy.** Not only should you focus on eating more healthy fats, but you also need to make sure you get enough fruits, vegetables, and other food groups.

3. **Getting enough sleep.** As an adult, you should get at least seven hours of good sleep every night, though many doctors state getting eight is better.

4. **Exercising.** You don't need to exercise for two hours every day, but you should set aside at least half an hour to exercise throughout your day. The least amount of time you should exercise twice a week is 20 minutes. For instance, some of the best exercise you can take part in is going for a 20-minute walk.

For most people, the hardest part of developing self-discipline is changing their habits. Fortunately, the more consistent you are with your new habits, the easier they are to change. In reality, it only takes a few days to a week to get into better habits, as long as you are consistent and remain focused on your habit.

One of the ways to change an unhealthy habit is to replace it with a healthier habit. For example, if you find yourself snacking on chips throughout the day, you can change your snack to something healthier, such as carrots, apples, or oranges. If you struggle to get to bed at a decent time and not getting enough sleep throughout the night, get up earlier in the morning. This will make you more tired at the end of the day and you will find yourself going to bed earlier.

Always remember to talk to yourself in a compassionate manner when you are focusing on change. If you don't follow through with your change one day, don't become frustrated with yourself. Forgive yourself and get in the mindset that tomorrow is a new day.

If you know that your unhealthy habits are the result of stress, you need to find ways to decrease some of your stress as this will help you stay more focused on healthy habits. Sometimes eliminating stress is a mindset change. You need to look at your stress as an avenue for growth and opportunity instead of work that must be done. Other times, you need to make some other lifestyle changes to help yourself decrease your stress.

Conclusion

By now, you might feel that your mind is overloaded with various tips and strategies to help you become a master of self-discipline. It is important that you don't let all this information overwhelm you. Always remember that you will take everything step by step and you can go as slow as you need to. As people often say, slow and steady wins the race!

The contents of this book not only help you learn what self-discipline is, but you also learned how to improve your self-discipline. You know the difference between self-esteem and self-confidence and how each ties into self-discipline. You know how to meditate, become more mindful, and focus on changing your habits by replacing unhealthy habits with healthy ones. You also understand that you need to control your mind by maintaining focus.

Some of the key points from this book you need to remember every day is as follows:

Always speak to yourself in a compassionate manner. You should give yourself the same respect and care that you give your best friend. If you wouldn't say something to someone else, why would you say it to yourself? Don't put yourself down by letting your inner critic take control.

Working toward mastering your self-discipline will be draining. There are times you will feel exhausted and not sure you can continue. Take a break and allow yourself time to breathe. Then, continue focusing on your plan and reaching your goal.

Never be afraid of failure. Fall forward and allow failure to help you grow.

Learn from your mistakes and move on.

Always remember that 'no' is a sentence all by itself. You do not have to give people a reason to why you can't take on extra work.

Put yourself first as your mental and emotional health is important.

Always take time to ensure you have some 'me time' during your day as this will help you maintain a calm environment.

Use the SMART rule when creating goals and write down your goals. Make sure that you have little steps to help you reach your goals.

Remember that learning is a constant part of your life. If you are smart, you will never stop learning.

No matter what you do, never give up. You are a strong person and you will succeed in your mission to become a master of self-discipline.

Overthinking

Control your thoughts, think positive & master your mindset.

How to manage stress with intentional thinking, positive self-talk and mindfulness meditation.

Introduction

What if I said something wrong? What if I did something wrong? What if they don't like me? Why did they say that? Why did that happen and what does it mean? Thinking makes you a human but thinking about something endlessly, in circles, might be exhausting. Your brain is designed to help you solve problems and see your way out of danger, but at times the wiring can be off or downright wrong and all of these thoughts become multiplied, and you obsess and mull and ruminate over every little nuance that was said or not said. It leaves you consumed, and the problems go unsolved. You spin round and round as if you are on a hamster wheel with the problem not solving itself. All this overthinking can ruin your day and your nights, which, in turn, will disrupt your sleep patterns and can affect your daily life and the pattern repeats over and over.

Nowadays, in the age of technology overload, there is evidence that we are reaching our limits as to what we can mentally handle. A few years ago, a study was conducted at the University of California-San Diego which found that each day people are being bombarded with the equivalent of 34gb of data and images. That's enough to crash an average laptop within a week. It's no wonder we are seeing more anxiety, depression, and mental breakdowns than any other generation before us.

Between our smartphones, internet, podcasts, social media, and emails, to name just a few, we are overwhelmed with approximately 105,000 words each day. While we may not be able to actually read that much in one day, it is what we are consuming even on a subconscious level. Our brains are having a hard time processing all this information. That is why mental health issues are on the rise. We are simply overwhelmed.

Caught up in this web of 'stuff' is the need to "keep up with Joneses." If the neighbor has it then you need it, which is hurting us physically and mentally. Not only are we collecting more material 'things,' but we are collecting more mental 'things.'

Doctors and scientists are just now coming to understand how important our mental health is in every other area of our lives. The idea of streamlining our lives and our thoughts is becoming imperative to our well-being. The most important streamlining we must do is on the inside before it can manifest on the outside. We need to become more aware of our thoughts and how to control them. That's not to say we stop to feel or think, but that we become more aware of why we are thinking about what we are. Become more aware of how it affects us. Become more aware of what serves us, what doesn't, and when to cut loose those thoughts or people from our lives that do not contribute to our well-being.

Congratulations for grabbing this book and welcome to walk through what overthinking is, how it can harm your mental health and happiness, and learn to take back the power of your brain to harness your thoughts from negative to positive and start to truly live a mindful, positive, and happy life.

Part 1: Theory

"Overthinking, also, best known as creating problems that are never there"

~David Sikhosana~

Chapter 1: Mental Clutters

"Nothing can harm you as much as your own thoughts unguarded."

– Buddha

Mental Clutter - what is it? What does it mean? It refers to the mind is too full of thoughts, which makes it difficult to process them all. When there are too many thoughts you can fall into a spiral of where to start. It can affect your ability to move or think. You start to tell yourself that you can't do it all, you're not worthy, what's the point of even starting, etc.

Mental clutter can be seen and felt in many forms, from simply having an overactive brain that can't grasp a handle on the various situations that arise daily just from living to what your house and work life is like.

Do you come home and see a kitchen counter cluttered with appliances, dishes, and strewn about mail? Then the task of getting it clean and shiny will be so overwhelming that you won't even start to tidy up or clear the 'clutter.' If you are constantly coming home to a cluttered home with 'stuff,' it can make your internal world feel cluttered. If you go to work and your desk is always cluttered with papers and other paraphernalia, it may feel hard to get organized and get a handle on your daily workload.

The other insidious part of clutter, whether mental or external, is our attachment to it, which can make getting rid of both the physical clutter and the mental clutter and thought patterns associated with it difficult to get rid of as we tend to see them as an extension of ourselves.

"A negative mind will never give you a positive life."

Google It

As a Gen X'er, I remember a time before Google when you had to run to the library if you were unsure of something, or you had to rely on friends and family's experiences to help you solve an argument or make a decision.

But today, if we are unable to find the answers we need within our own mind or our collective hive of friends and family, there is always Google. There is a plethora of knowledge and information at our fingertips these days that you would think would make our decision-making easier. However, decisions are getting harder and harder to make because now we can weigh all the pros and cons of every option available to us, and a simple query on Google can send us down a rabbit hole of clicking. Before we know it, hours may have gone by or we've become distracted by something else that we forgot what we were searching for in the first place.

All this information isn't empowering us as it should; it's overwhelming us. All this access to unlimited information is causing us to have greater fears about making the wrong decisions. It doesn't help that our attention span for such things is dropping for each subsequent generation that comes after Gen X. Millennials have a whopping 12-second attention span and Gen Z is even lower at eight seconds, compared to Baby Boomers who have an attention span of approximately 12 minutes. This doesn't bode well for anxiety and depression when combined with too much information at our fingertips.

That's what I like to call analysis paralysis, when presented with too many options it's easy to say, "I can't" or "I don't have time to" and fill in the blank. A lot of times it's simply because we don't want to make a decision, but there are cases where the number of options simply becomes too overwhelming and anxiety-producing to deal with and what is seen as procrastination is more overwhelming.

How many times have you decided that you wanted to do something, let's say renovate a room in your house or go on a family vacation, but when you started to research the different colors of paint, flooring or tile swatches, and fabric options for slipcovers or curtains or looking at hotels and excursion options or flights you just threw up your hands and said forget it? Analysis paralysis, too many choices. In this instance, I recommend starting with one piece of the puzzle. Figure out the theme of the room first and even if this feels daunting, then consider getting quotes and ideas from a professional; these are usually free. For vacations, start with a time of day you would like to leave and how many layovers you can handle on your way to the destination, then start narrowing down the flights. Once that is sorted out, you can work on hotels and things to do.

Thinking of it in bite-sized, snackable pieces will help reduce the overwhelm.

Less is more

The more choices we have, the more stressed we become. Less is definitely more when it comes to our brains and overthinking.

Studies in neuroscience and psychology have been showing that analysis paralysis takes a far greater toll on us than we thought. It affects our productivity and well-being more than just being a time suck.

Overthinking lowers our performance on mentally demanding tasks. High-level cognitive tasks require what is called our working memory. This is our short-term memory system that has a limited amount of information for whatever task we have at hand, basic or complicated, and prevents us from being distracted while performing this task. Our working memory is what allows us to focus on the information we need to access to get things done at the moment that we need to do them. Access to this information is limited, and if we are constantly distracted or disrupted then our performance will suffer. However, when we worry or overthink it takes up vital 'retail' space in our brain, and we can no longer efficiently process the information needed to make the important decisions. We simply have a limited supply of working memory, similar to a computer hard drive, and once it's used up, we can't store anymore.

You will find that with repeated high-pressure stress and anxiety-producing situations where you rely on your working memory, your cognitive ability to perform these tasks will suffer. The harder you try to perform the tasks, the more your performance will suffer.

Researchers believe that the anxiety about the situation is what produces the working memory to have distracting thoughts. It's so busy with these distracting thoughts that it can no longer assist you with performing the task at hand, which then causes your productivity to plummet even lower.

In these situations, it is best to try and declutter your mind. While this can be easier said than done, the state of our mental health depends on it. I will say this again and again throughout this book, awareness is key to what you are thinking, what you are telling yourself and how you are reacting to stressful situations.

You can't keep rehashing the past or rehearsing the future. There are no shortcuts to get rid of negative, unwanted thoughts, but there are ways to develop a minimalist mindset.

When stuck in a vicious downward spiral of rumination, it's helpful to emphasize helping others. Consider volunteering your time to help the elderly or terminally sick. It's so easy to get caught up in our day-to-day thoughts and problems and stress about all the ways things can go wrong. But the reality is that there are others who have it much worse than you do. Overthinking eats away at our willpower - willpower is similar to a muscle, the more use it gets, the more tired it will become. Menial tasks, such as brushing our teeth, take up little willpower, but the more we agonize over a decision, the more we deplete our reserve of willpower, which leads to feeling exhausted and overwhelmed. In this state, we are unable to properly assess situations and we are more likely to choose unwisely - unhealthy snacks, skipping exercise, parking our butts on the couch to watch TV instead of healthy food, exercise, and maybe working on that side project that has been calling to us. Consider decluttering your physical world to help your mental world. We are so consumed with accumulating things, but each new thing gives us something else to think about, worry about, or feel guilt over because we know we didn't really need that thing in the first place. In the house, less is definitely more. Overthinking makes us less happy - Economist Herman Simon coined the phrase 'satisficer' in 1956 to describe a decision-making style that "prioritizes an adequate solution over an optimal solution." The flip side of the satisficer is the 'maximizer.' These people are not happy with good enough; it has to be the best and they will exhaust *all* possibilities before making a decision *if* they can come to one that is.

Common phrases from a maximizer might be "It can't hurt to look" or "I won't settle for second best." But in trying to make the best possible decision and avoid making a 'bad' one, they often don't make a decision at all. Then the regret, self-blame, and anxiousness kicks in. Because of these, maximizers tend to be less happy, have lower self-esteem, and more regrets that those of us who are satisficers.

The more options they have to make these decisions, the worse they feel and the more they try to make the right decision, the less likely they are to be happy with the results when they finally decide. For a maximizer, less choice is the better option. For example, let's say you are getting married and you want the perfect necklace and earring set. So, you head to Etsy to start searching through the pages. You find some that are nice and would probably suffice, but you feel that they're just not perfect enough, so you keep scrolling and looking through the artists' pages. Before you know it, you have looked at over 50 pages of jewelry and not found the 'perfect' pair. Now you are overwhelmed and annoyed that you haven't picked anything, so you walk away and decided not to pick anything at all. A satisficer would probably have settled on the first pair, deciding it met most of the criteria they had set and been happy with their purchase. As you can see the maximizer was not satisfied with any of the options and subsequently didn't get anything. Last, but not least, is simply slowing down. Take brain breaks when you need to. A calmer, less-cluttered mind is harder to wind up with anxious thoughts of the past or the future.

Technology

One huge mental clutter that weighs heavily on people today is technology. There aren't many of us that might remember a time before Google and cell phones, but I do and there are days when I long for the pure, old times.

The smartphone and being connected at all hours have become so prevalent that it is like a drug, and it can become an addiction. When we don't get that rush of dopamine from checking our social feeds, reading the news and posting photos of our lives we go into withdrawal. It's become the digital equivalent of "keeping up with Joneses." How many times have you gone out for coffee with a friend or out to dinner with your spouse and they keep checking their phones during the midst of a conversation with you? I know I do it too and I'm guilty of doing it. But what is it costing us?

The pings and beeps from our notifications, seeing the carefully curated Instagram accounts or Facebook posts can send us into a spiral of comparisons because our lives aren't as 'perfect' as our friends or neighbors or celebrities or even the guy down the street. This comparing of lives can contribute to lower self-esteem, especially in younger adults or teens. Feelings of feeling inferior to their peers, that their peers are more successful and happier than they are. What gets forgotten is that most people don't like to admit that life can get messy so they only post the 'perfect' shot or image of whatever is going on in their life, so what we are comparing ourselves to is the image they want others to believe about their lives, not their actual real life.

We check our phones at night, disturbing our sleep patterns. We check our emails and social feeds before we've even had breakfast and then start the day harried, angry, and depressed before we've even set foot out the door to work or school. Is it a wonder we are constantly worrying and overthinking about every detail?

We're so focused on what's going on online "out there" that we are missing being present with what's right in front of us. Family, friends, and kids all of these need us to be present, and we're missing because we're too busy worrying about the past or the future.

We need to take the time to unplug, put the phone away, and take the time to recharge. But what do you do when you really can't? What if you work for yourself and your business is primarily online? Well, then I say, you need to become more intentional with your time online. Having a business online doesn't mean you need to be attached 24/7.

I would argue that the reason you decided to work for yourself was so that you could spend more time with family and friends, but are you really spending more time with them if you're constantly attached to your phone? You may be home with them or able to catch up over coffee but if you're constantly looking at your phone, you're not being present with those right in front of you.

My wakeup call was when my three-year-old son told me to put my phone away one day. I realized that if he was telling me to put it away at such a young age, then I was spending far too much time on it. That was when I decided to institute the "blackout" periods. From the time I picked him up from preschool until he went to bed, I wouldn't handle my phone at all. After some time, I noticed that his temper tantrums and outbursts diminished and so did my stress levels around these outbursts. Putting down my phone has improved our relationship.

I know it can be tough, but I recommend at least trying to put the phone down or putting it on airplane mode for an hour or two and work your times up from there. Let people know that you're doing this, so you don't go back to multiple texts from people wondering where you are and checking to see if you're okay. Seeing that many messages could become stressful and overwhelming in and of itself. Consider leaving the phone at home on a weekend when you're running errands. I have done this accidentally when I forgot I was charging it and found that I didn't miss having it.

Chapter 2: Overthinking

"Worrying is like sitting in a rocking chair. It gives you something to do but it doesn't get you anywhere."

- English Proverb

What is overthinking? How do you tell if you're an overthinker?

Do you find yourself constantly running around in circles either thinking the same thought over and over or analyzing it ad nauseam? Or possibly thinking multiple thoughts that you just can't focus on one and then become paralyzed by all the thoughts. That is overthinking.

Do you struggle with decisions? Too many decisions? Too many ideas? Not able to make a decision? Analysis paralysis is the other side of overthinking.

Psychologist Barry Schwartz coined the term "Paradox of Choice," which sums up our technological age perfectly. With greater choices, which really should make our lives easier, it is actually leading to greater anxiety, indecision, and paralysis, which in turn leads to a greater fear of making the wrong decision.

Overthinking can kill your creativity. Not only does overthinking impede your ability to perform high-level cognitive tasks, but it also impedes your ability to think creatively. It limits our creative potential. When we are stuck in this pattern, it is almost impossible to think "outside the box."

Overthinking has roots in other disorders, but by itself is not specifically a documented disorder. Overthinking is common and is a symptom in many other disorders such as anxiety, depression, PTSD, panic disorder, social anxiety disorder, and various other disorders.

Seriously, who doesn't go a day without worrying or over-thinking about something? But does this thinking rule your mind? Overthinking is excessive thinking about something that causes you anxiety, stress, or fear. It's not just about thinking about something too much, it's obsessing about it, to the point that it starts to affect your life. To worry about your family's safety, for example, and overthink on other issues is completely normal. I believe we all need to worry about and overthink from time to time, it's how we learn and grow. Normally, you would wonder or worry about an issue, you would ponder it for a time, then let it go and move on with your day. With overthinking this is all you can do. While you may not think about the same thing all the time, you will always find something to worry and obsess about.

When these thoughts become obsessive and disruptive and start to affect your ability to live life, it's time to consider alternative options to cope or to seek some professional help.

Are You an Overthinker?

How many nights do you find yourself lying in bed and your brain is just spinning on the hamster wheel around and around?

Do you constantly question why you said or did something and then worry about it for hours, days, weeks or longer?

The hard part is really looking at what you do, why you do it, and then catching yourself in the act so that you can start to correct it. Especially when you are caught in the middle of an episode. Our brain has a wonderful way of trying to protect us, some call this the ego, and in protecting us it tells that only we can solve the problem so it keeps us going around and around trying to solve something that is most likely unsolvable on our own. But in telling us that we can solve it ourselves we are perpetuation the overthinking analysis of each and every problem that occurs.

Here are some signs that you might be an overthinker:

- I have difficulty sleeping because my brain won't shut off.
- I constantly ask myself a lot of "what if..." questions.
- I continually compare myself to others.
- I constantly relive past failures and mistakes over and over.
- I spend a lot of time worrying about things I have no control over, like the future.
- I relive past traumas (such as abuse or the death of a loved one).

The biggest part of overthinking is the worry over things that have happened in the past or that we have no control over as well as thinking about future events that haven't even happened yet, so we have no idea how they occur. Constantly running these things around in our brains without finding a solution to them is futile.

There are various types of overthinking, and none of them are very helpful and they can be quite destructive. I will cover some of them in a later chapter for you to get an understanding of what you may be doing, and then in Part 2, I will provide some tips, tricks, and ideas on how to combat them.

Why Do We Overthink?

The interesting thing about our brain is that the recall of negative experiences is easier because of how the memory is processed within our brain. Scientists believe that it is easier to recall because of how the experience affects us. It doesn't mean we're all pessimists just waiting for the ball to drop, but it does mean that recalling the negative memories are kept in a more accessible part of our brain.

Our hardwiring will make us more susceptible to recall the negative experiences over positive ones. Did you suffer childhood abuse? Did your parents always yell at you or tell you that you weren't good enough? Did you witness a trauma? These experiences will hardwire you see the negative before you even consider the positive.

The reason for this is a chemical in our brain called cortisol. It flows freely and is more easily accessed than its counterpart dopamine. Cortisol spurs on the negative thoughts that our brains *love!* This is our danger is an imminent warning system. The problem occurs when we constantly operator from this state of mind.

The reality is that most of the problems that arise, that provide the rush of cortisol, are very rarely life or death situations that require us to constantly be thinking in the negative, but when we live in this state for too long our brains start to prefer this pattern because thinking negatively is easier. However, this can become extremely detrimental to our health and well-being.

Overthinking has a strong link to procrastination and perfectionism. Consider this, do you have to move things around your desk or your home to accomplish certain tasks? So maybe you look at the clutter and start to think maybe you should tidy up, but then wonder where the heck to start, so you turn away and ignore it. Do you often end up not doing something because you think you'll be good at it? You don't want to fail so why should you even start? Is there a hobby or something you would like to try but fear looking like a fool because you might make a mistake?

Ignoring the problem can then produce more cortisol, which then simply makes us feel bad and on edge about all the perceived work it would take to clean up the mess. This is particularly true for women.

Now you also need to understand that your level of overthinking and clutter will not always be the same as the person next to you on the subway. But in any case, clutter is clutter and can start to impede your mental health with all the 'clutter' in your life.

Overthinking and mental health is a little like the chicken or the egg scenario. Which came first, the anxiety and depression that can trigger the overthinking or overthinking that can cause anxiety and depression? It has been linked to psychological problems such as depression and anxiety, probably because overthinking can cause mental decline and as your mental health declines you are more likely to continue the overthinking and then the dark downward spiral happens and it becomes a vicious cycle that starts to become almost impossible to get out.

Now it's not all doom and gloom, many good positive experiences can overcome all the bad, negative ones, but they are harder to recall, and they definitely take more work. Do you catch yourself constantly looking at your phone for a text from a friend or your significant other? You are looking for that hit of dopamine to feel better, there is a rush in receiving a positive word or something encouraging from those we love. But barring that external validation you will need to work on developing new patterns and ways of thinking to counter all that cortisol.

Procrastination versus Perfectionism

Procrastination is defined as chronically avoiding difficult tasks and situations and deliberately looking for distractions so as not to complete the tasks even knowing that avoiding these situations could have negative outcomes.

Perfectionism is defined as by a person's striving for flawlessness and setting high-performance standards, accompanied by critical self-evaluations.

Perfectionists are often procrastinators because psychologically it is more acceptable to them to never start a task or project than to face the prospect of failing at it or falling short of the expected performance.

Have you ever said or heard someone say they perform better under pressure? Research shows that this is not usually the case, usually, it is their way of putting off whatever task or chore needs to be done.

Have you ever told yourself you just don't feel like doing something? When you tell yourself this, what you are really saying is "I don't prioritize this" or "I'm not going to do this, because I'm afraid of failing."

While most people would agree that a certain level of high standards is appropriate to push ourselves to always do our best, perfectionism is more about setting such high standards that they either can't be met or can be met but with great difficulty, and even then, if the standards are met a perfectionist will still find a flaw in the way it was accomplished.

Perfectionism is a one-way ticket to unhappiness. You are constantly striving for the impossible, then beating yourself up for not meeting your own expectations. Life is conditional based on flawless performances that no one can live up to.

There are three types of procrastinators and perfectionists:

- **Thrill-seekers** - these procrastinators get a rush from last-minute planning or deadlines

- **Avoiders** - these procrastinators put off tasks for fear of failure or making mistakes or potentially putting it off for fear of failure

- **Decisional** - these procrastinators struggle to make decisions, thereby telling themselves that by not making a decision they are absolving themselves of responsibility for the outcome of any given event

- **Self-imposed perfectionists** - impose unrealistic expectations on themselves

- **Other-imposed perfectionists** - impose unrealistic expectations on others

- **Socially prescribed perfectionists** - perceiving unrealistic expectations from others

Wherever you may fall on the spectrum there is a positive side to this and that is with a little effort and some work you can overcome both perfectionism and procrastination. Recognizing your patterns and triggers will help you on the road to correcting these issues and learning to appreciate the messiness of life and all its flaws.

Chapter 3: Mindset

"It does not matter how slow you go as long as you do not stop."

– Confucius

E verything starts with a mindset. But you might be asking yourself, what is that exactly? This boils down to whether you believe qualities such as intelligence is fixed or changeable.

"I'm not physically gifted to run a 10k run."

There are two types of mindsets - fixed and growth. People with a fixed mindset believe that certain traits are inborn, fixed and that they are unchangeable. People with a growth mindset believe that these same abilities can be developed, changed, and strengthened with work.

Your mindset plays a critical role in how you handle things that occur in your life. Do you see everything as a problem that can't be solved, or do you see the problem as a challenge to be solved?

This mindset generally develops early in childhood and is based on the way you were raised. That's not to say that it can't be changed, but it will be difficult. Changing years of conditioning will be a challenge but worth it in the end. However, since you are now reading this book is a good sign you want to improve. So, let's start at the beginning to make you understand:

Fixed mindset:

- As a child, you were probably told to focus on smarts and excelling academically instead of loving the idea of learning.
- You were probably told to focus more on how others perceived or judged you, so you feared that you weren't living up to expectations.

Growth mindset:

- As a child, you were encouraged to explore and learn, to make mistakes and embrace new experiences.
- Rather than seeing those mistakes as setbacks, you were encouraged to see them as learning opportunities and therefore try new things to explore your potential.

Where do you fall into this spectrum?

Wherever you fall into, it's important to understand that you want to focus on the outcome of the issue as opposed to the whole process. It doesn't matter how you get to your end goal, all that matters is you try, and if you make a mistake along the way or stumble off your path, that's okay. The how is almost irrelevant compared with the why. The how will take care of itself as you move along. It's the why that will keep you going to try and get to your desired result. When you stumble, know, that it's okay. Get up, dust yourself off, and try again.

Control Your Thoughts

If you haven't figured it out by now, your mind is a powerful, intricate machine that can be used for good in your life, but it can also be quite destructive.

Your mind and your thoughts affect all your perceptions and interpretations of your world and reality, they also affect your mood, whether you are conscious of that or not. So why let it run amok?

Your mind, your thoughts. So, let's take back the power.

The average human brain thinks between 50,000 and 80,000 thoughts a day, which translates into approximately 2,000 to 3,300 thoughts per hour. That's amazing! But what if most of those thoughts are negative? Then it's no wonder we get overwhelmed and anxious. Then we start to feel unproductive and self-abuse ourselves.

Let's start to make those thoughts positive instead of negative. Most of the time, you probably won't even realize what you're thinking; you're on autopilot. But you are aware of the impact these thoughts have on you because you're depressed, anxious, lonely, sad, etc.

But what if the opposite could be true? How would it feel if you could control what you thought throughout the day? Because your thoughts are also responsible for why you laugh, smile, etc.

Well, guess what? You can!

Sometimes identifying the feeling is the best you can do at any given moment. Well, that's a start. Why do you feel that way? Work backward. What happened to precipitate the feeling? Once you identify the event that jump-started the feeling try to dig deeper. Why did this elicit the feeling it did? A lot of the time this is just the event that brought about the feeling isn't always the root cause of the feeling, but it's enough to start the anxiety or anger or whatever feeling you're experiencing.

Think of it this way, right now with all the negative thoughts swirling around in there, you have 'squatters' living rent-free. It's time to evict them.

These 'squatters' are known as the:

- The Inner Critic
- The Worrier
- The Reactor

How You Can Master Your Mind

You need to not only think about your thoughts but observe them. You must pay attention to the thought(s) so you can identify which one(s) are running the show. Then we know who to evict.

The Inner Critic

The Inner Critic berates, puts down, etc. When you notice it's starting up, interrupt it.

Yell "Stop it!" out loud or if that feels strange then just yell it in your mind. "No!" "Enough!" or whatever works to stop the flow of berating, then counter it with the opposite thought or an "I am" affirmation.

If your Inner Critic likes to tell you that you're ugly, then replace it with "I am a beautiful creature of the universe" or "I am magnificent" or "I'm beautiful as I am and love and accept myself as I am." Come up with your own that resonates with you to stop the flow of negative thoughts.

You can also try to discredit whatever sentiment is coming up. "Just because so and so said anything, it doesn't have to be true. It is just their opinion, not a fact."

The Inner Critic is the worst renter to set up shop, so evicting this one first will be difficult but will also make evicting the other renters that much easier as this renter also instigates and incites the others.

The Worrier

A worrying thought is easily identified by how it makes you feel. Your fight or flight response will kick in, your heart rate will increase, breathing will become, palms become sweaty, your stomach with feel like it has butterflies, and your muscles tense up.

The Worrier comes to live with prolonged anxiety.

Use the same interruption pattern as above for the inner critic but instead replace the thoughts with ones of gratitude for the outcome you desire.

Whether you believe in a higher power or not, praying to something bigger than yourself helps calm the brain and manifest the desired result. Myself, I don't necessarily believe in God, but I do believe in something bigger than myself, so I tend to pray to source or the universe.

"Thank you, universe, for granting me the strength and resilience to see this issue as a challenge and rise above it. Thank you for giving me the insight to see that the situation is not as bad as I have perceived and that everything will work out."

Be as happy as you can while saying this, try smiling inwardly and outwardly. It will feel weird to begin with, but consistency will make it feel natural. Always make your statements in the present tense.

If you can visualize the outcome and the feelings you want behind it, visualizing can enhance the experience and the feelings. I will be talking more about visualizations in a later chapter.

Doing this will help take the steam out of the Reactor.

The Reactor

The Reactor is similar to the worrier, only this tenant engages your fight or flight mode, so it will take a bit more time and conscious awareness to evict or eradicate.

The Reactor comes out when you have been triggered, so coming to understand your triggers, why you become triggered, and when will help with this tenant. When you feel those old feelings of fear, anxiety, anger, or pain arise then you can start the process of interrupting the pattern.

Conscious breathing is one way to slow the Reactor and eventually eliminate it. It's as simple as it sounds, you just become very conscious of your breathing. Pay attention to your in and out breaths. Become conscious of the air entering your nostrils, feeling your lungs fill and expand, and focus on your belly rising. Breathe out through your nose *not* your mouth, noticing your lungs deflate and your belly falling; concentrate on the air leaving your nostrils.

Another way to do this, which I prefer, is to count. Breathe in for a count of four, five or six, whichever feels more comfortable for you and will fill your lungs, then hold that breath for the same count if you can. Then breathe out for longer to expel all the air from your lungs. So, if you breathe in and hold for a count of five, try expelling the air in a count of six or seven.

Repeat either of these for as long as you like or until you feel your body and mind start to normalize.

Master this and you will have evicted one of your more difficult tenants.

Law of Attraction (LOA)

Have you ever thought about something or someone when suddenly it or he has appeared, or the phone rings and that person is on the other end? O have you thought of someone and bumped into them randomly on the street?

It wasn't random, this is the power of your mind and the Law of Attraction.

In its simplest form, the Law of Attraction, or LOA, means to attract into our lives whatever you are focusing on. LOA uses the power of your mind to materialize your thoughts, dreams, and desires into reality.

All thoughts turn into things, eventually. Doesn't matter whether it's a good thought or bad, it will manifest into something at some point.

If all you ever focus on is doom and gloom then that is all that will be in your life, but if you focus on positive thoughts, goals, and dreams that you want to achieve then you will and the universe will find a way to make them happen.

Now, to be clear, LOA isn't about just thinking a thought and sitting back and waiting for the universe to magically bring it to you. You do need to take some action toward your goal. Once you start taking action, whether it's massive action or just small, consistent steps, the universe will open doors and bring you opportunities if you are willing to see them will help you on your journey to reach your goal.

However, recognizing and accepting the Law of Attraction is to acknowledge that every decision you have made, good or bad, has shaped you and the direction your life has taken. While this might be a hard pill to swallow, it should also be noted that now you know differently and can start to reshape your life and reality.

Rejoice in being liberated to know the difference. Rejoice in the realization that we truly are the creators of our lives.

Rejoice in the knowledge that the universe truly does have our backs!

Our lives are blank canvases and we've been painting pictures based on what we want, what we dream of and what has happened but what if you don't like the picture anymore?

Change it!

That is the joy of life and the Law of Attraction.

Start picturing and painting a new canvas. Pick new images, new feelings. Hold the image in your mind's eye, feel the feelings. As long as you are willing to put in some effort toward your new goals, write them down in your phone, on scrap pieces of paper, or in a journal specifically for this purpose. Then watch the Law of Attraction take over.

Mental Health and Law of Attraction

While the Law of Attraction isn't a substitute for a healthy diet and exercise, it can assist with keeping your mental health clean in training your brain to see the positive in everything and promoting positive thoughts instead of negative, which in turn can improve your physical health.

Learning to take time for self-care can go a long way to decreasing levels of stress, which will assist with better clarity and mental health. This will help in releasing the feelings of doubt and unworthiness and direct your thoughts to more confidence and faith in the universe. As stated earlier, the brain doesn't always know the difference between what's real and what's our imagination. So when you focus on the things that you don't want like being in poor health, being angry at our kids or feeling anxious all the time, what you are telling your brain is that these are the things that you really *do* want.

You are operating in a lack of mentality by constantly worrying about the things you don't have. So for the Law of Attraction to start working in the positive for you, you will need to start focusing on the things you truly do want, like excellent health, being calmer with your kids, and no longer feeling anxious when something occurs.

I have found that setting it and forgetting is when the Law of Attraction is the strongest, simply because I'm no longer worried about what I don't have. I know that eventually whatever it is will make its way to me and as almost as soon as I have forgotten that I asked for 'x,' it comes to me and is usually quite a nice surprise.

To practice the Law of Attraction, consider starting small, with something that you would like, but you aren't particularly attached to. Sit in a space that is quiet for a few minutes or as long as you can spare, close your eyes, in your mind's eye start to picture this 'thing' that you would like. It doesn't matter what it is, just as long as you can see it, feel it, imagine it is yours and what that will feel like when you acquire this 'thing.' Hold the image, get as crystal clear as you can on this image; the more detail you can draw into the image, the better. Once you are done, thank the universe for sending this to you and release the image. Then go about your day, knowing it is on its way to you.

Keep practicing on manifesting small things that you would like, and as you start to see the power of the Law of Attraction start asking for slightly larger things. Never attach too much significance to these things as that will tell the universe that you are lacking, which will block you from receiving your desired object.

As you practice the Law of Attraction more and more your confidence will grow, and you will begin to see the power of your mind and all that the universe has to offer.

Chapter 4: Stress Management

"One of the best pieces of advice I ever got was from a horse master.
He told me to go slow to go fast. I think that applies to everything in
life. We live as though there aren't enough hours in the day but if we
do each thing calmly and carefully, we will get it done quicker and
with much less stress."

- Viggo Mortensen

L earning good stress management techniques is key to understanding and managing your stress levels, which in turn will help you manage your anxiety and any other underlying issues you may be experiencing.

Stress management is "a set of techniques intended to help people deal more effectively with their stress loads." It's about taking charge of your life, lifestyle, thoughts, emotions, and how you deal with problems.

Let's be real, in this day and age with all the technology at our fingertips one would hope that our stress levels would decrease, but it has been shown that stress among people is at an all-time high. There will always be bills to pay, work and family responsibilities, and there will never feel like are enough hours in the day, but understanding that you are, in fact, in control of your life is the foundation of good stress management.

Stress can wreak havoc on your emotional well-being, your health, and your thought processes, especially high levels of stress. Simply put, it narrows your ability to think clearly, function effectively, and enjoy life.

There is a lot of pressure on people these days to multitask, and the more you can multitask, the more capable you seem. But I believe that multitasking is a bad word and one that should be stricken from our vocabulary. I feel that multitasking adds to our stress level because when we take on too much and aren't able to complete a task or get pulled in too many directions, that's when our focus fractures and we start to feel like we're failures or incompetent because we can't ever seem to get anything done. If we simply focused on one task until it was completed, then we would feel accomplished and could move on to the next. I realize in some cases this is not always possible to do, but I believe we need to minimize distractions as much as possible to minimize our stress.

Effective stress management deals with this; it helps us break the hold that stress has on our lives so that we can be happier, healthier, and much more productive. It allows us the opportunity to have more balance in our lives.

I believe, there is magic in a little bit of chaos. That is life. but there should never be chaos in your mind. You should still be able to find time for work, friends, family, relaxation, and fun. Effective stress management will help you break down the stress that chaos might have created in your life, so you can be happier, healthier and more productive. Effective stress management will provide you with the resilience to hold up when under pressure.

Tips for Handling Stress

Stress management is not a one size fits all. You need to discover what your stressors are and then discover the right tools that will work for you.

- Identify the sources of stress in your life - there will always be obvious 'big' stressors, such as moving, changing jobs or careers or maybe going through a divorce, but it's the smaller, less obvious stressor that can be complicated to pinpoint. To identify, you must look closely at your habits, your attitude and any excuses you know you tell yourself. Maybe you procrastinate on almost everything, telling yourself that you're just too busy to complete the task, yet it really bothers you that the task isn't completed. Why? What is holding you back from completing it? How would it feel to knuckle under and complete the task to get it off your to-do list? Until you cannot accept responsibility for the role you are playing, in creating and maintaining the stress levels in your life, you won't be able to change the level of your stress.

Our response to stress is automatic, but some stressors will arise at predictable times. When you know they are going to happen, then you can consider avoiding, altering, adapting or accepting the situation.

Avoiding unnecessary stress

There will be times when it's best to avoid a situation. You're not necessarily hiding from the problem; you are simply avoiding a situation that you know will be detrimental to your well-being.

* **Learn to say 'no'** - knowing your limits and when to say no will go a long way to diminishing your stress. It's okay to not accept every lunch invite with colleagues or party invitation that comes along.

* **Avoid people you know are stressing you** - we all have that one friend, who we've known for so long, that there is a level of loyalty or obligation to talk to them or hanging out with them, but they really stress us out every time we

get together. It's okay not to talk to them all the time. It's okay to set that boundary.

* **Take control of your environment** - do you tense up every time you walk in the front door because of all the clutter? Start setting aside time to purge. Throw it out, donate it or sell it.

Alter the situation

If you can't avoid a stressful situation, then consider altering the situation itself or your reaction to it.

* **Express your feelings** - instead of bottling them up. Be assertive and communicate your feelings or concerns to those who need to hear it, but be respectful.

* **Compromise -** if you are asking someone to change their ways, then be prepared to do the same.

* **Try to find some balance in the chaos** - there is something about slowing down and finding the right balance between all the obligations and the fun that you crave. Because only work and no play is a recipe for disaster and burnout.

Adapt to the stressor

If you can't change the situation, then consider adapting yourself to the situation. By changing your expectations and attitude you can regain some control over the situation and your stress.

* **Reframe your problems** - try to see them in a more positive light.

* **Look at the bigger picture** - will this issue matter in a year? In a month? Is it worth it to skip sleep?

* **Adjust your standards** - avoid perfectionism, learn to be okay with "good enough" for now. Once you have a handle on your stress if you feel you must raise your standards, then, by all means, do as long as it doesn't become a stressor again.

* **Accept what you cannot change** - there will be stressors you can avoid, that you can't alter or adapt to, but as difficult as it may seem you can accept them.

* **Stop trying to control the uncontrollable** - you can't control other people and what they will say or do, so instead of stressing out over it, focus on things such as your reaction to them.

* **Learn to forgive** - let go of any anger and resentment you have to a person or the situation. It can be difficult, but in

the long run, it frees you from the negative energy and allows you to move on.

* **Get moving** - moving is a huge stress reliever, even though it's probably the last thing you feel like doing. I have to admit movement and exercise was always the last thing on my mind when I was feeling overwhelmed or stressed. What I've been enjoying lately was cranking some music and dancing around my living room. A nice byproduct apart from the instant stress release, was that I have felt also more creative. However, if you don't feel like dancing, you can either take your dog for a walk, use the stairs instead of the elevator or just park your car a kilometer more away than usual.

• **Make time for fun and relaxation -** we get so busy that sometimes having fun falls to the bottom of the list. In this busy world, what is relaxation? There is far too much to do to be able to relax.

* **Schedule in your leisure time** - don't allow other obligations to get in the way. We schedule doctor appointments and time with our friends, why not schedule in some relaxation time. Then stick to it!

* **Keep your sense of humor -** there isn't much that a good laugh and a sense of humor can't cure. Always try to see the lighter side of things.

* **Take up a relaxation practice** - Yoga and meditation are wonderful for relaxing and calming the mind.

● **Maintain a healthy lifestyle**

* **Eat a healthy, balanced diet -** well-nourished bodies are better able to cope with stress, so be mindful of what you are eating. Maintain healthy food choices to keep your energy levels up, which will also regulate your emotions and moods.

* **Reduce your caffeine and sugar** - the 'rush' from sugar and caffeine is short-lived and the crash that happens afterward will affect your mood and energy levels. By reducing the amount of sugar and caffeine in your diet, you will find that you feel more relaxed and a nice byproduct of that is you will find you sleep better.

* **Avoid alcohol, cigarettes, and drugs** - using alcohol or drugs to escape from your issues is an easy out, but one that is only temporary. Self-medicating with these substances really only masks the problems you are facing. Don't avoid your problems, tackle them head-on, with a clear mind.

* **Get enough sleep** - getting adequate sleep not only rests your mind but your body as well. Feeling tired sucks, but also increases our chances of irritability which also increases irrational thinking.

Understanding Your Stress

High levels of cortisol can wear down the brain's ability to function properly. Basically, stress can kill your brain cells and even reduce the size of your brain. Cortisol is a natural hormone that occurs when stresses are triggered.

Chronic stress has been known to have a shrinking effect on the prefrontal cortex, which is the area responsible for memory and learning and at the same time can increase the size of the amygdala, which can make the brain more receptive to stress. This is through the overproduction of cortisol that the body then has trouble releasing. Cortisol is believed to create a domino effect that hard-wires pathways between the hippocampus and amygdala that could create a vicious cycle of a brain that is more predisposed to a "fight or flight" mode of thinking and reacting.

Stress can be a short-term event and as 'simple' as a fight with a loved one or it can be a recurring event such as managing a demanding job. Recurring events or conditions that are intense and sustained over long periods of time can be problematic due to the significant toll it can take on your body and brain, and that is can also promote inflammation, which will, over time, affect your heart health.

A byproduct of all this is the effect this has on the body and how toxic stress can impair the immune system and exacerbate any already existing illnesses. So, it's not always about calming an overactive mind, it's also about calming the body.

Glucose and the Brain

The brain depends on glucose as a fuel for functions such as thinking, memory, and learning. If this dips too low, then it can have an adverse effect on our neurotransmitters. If there isn't enough glucose in our brain, then these neurotransmitters aren't produced and communication between neurons breaks down, which will affect our attention, memory, and learning.

When we are tired, our brains release more of a hormone called ghrelin, which is a hunger hormone, and well-rested brains release more leptin, which is an appetite suppressant. Because what we eat can be largely influenced by our moods and how much sleep we got the night before, when we're stressed out, we tend to reach for high fat, sugary treats, which will increase our blood sugar levels and increase our insulin levels as our body tries to keep up balanced.

at becomes a vicious cycle because the more insulin our body creates the more it makes us hungry and then we tend to fill ourselves with empty sugary calories.

We need to learn to be more cognizant of what we are fueling our body with as well the amount of stress we encounter. Stress is a normal part of the human experience, but when it becomes chronic or constant that's when we need to take steps to minimize it.

Anxiety

"Our anxiety does not come from thinking about the future, but from wanting to control it."

- Khalil Gibran

Anxiety is the brain's natural response to stress and danger. The feeling of fear or apprehension for something that is about to come, unknowing of a situation, the unfamiliar, such as a job interview, your first day of school, having to take a test you feel unprepared for, etc. These are all normal and the feeling of anxiety can give you a bit of a boost and can motivate you to work harder or do better so that these feelings of anxiety don't arise anymore.

But when it starts to impact your life and lasts longer than six months, that when you may have a disorder. The biggest problem with anxiety is that demands you live in the past worrying about things that have already happened and there is nothing you can do to change them, and then demands you look to the future, worrying about things that haven't even happened so again, you have no control over what is to come.

In the case of a disorder, it can be intense at times and feel unexplainable, debilitating even. There may always be a feeling of fear with that feels irrational, but there doesn't seem to be anything you can do about it.

It may cause you to stop doing the things that you enjoy, and in extreme cases, it could prevent you from doing 'normal' everyday things, like cross a street or even leaving your house.

Every person will experience anxiety differently. Symptoms can range in number and severity, but they usually can start with feeling disconnected from your body and mind.

Some symptoms include:

- Increased heart rate
- Rapid breathing
- Butterflies in the stomach
- Difficulty sleeping

What causes anxiety?

There are no conclusive answers on why it happens or what the exact causes are, but scientists and researchers are now coming to believe that it is a combination of genetics, our environments, diet, and our brain chemistry.

Anxiety seems to occur alongside other mental health issues, such as depression and/or substance abuse. Alcohol, caffeine, nicotine, and other drugs used to try to ease the symptoms of anxiety can make the disorder worse because you are only masking the issues, not addressing them.

There are three areas of the brain that are affected by stress and anxiety:

Amygdala - which senses threats and alerts the brain to signs of danger. This can trigger a fear and anxiety response. It plays a role in fears that involve specific things such a fear of dogs or possibly drowning.

Hippocampus - can also affect anxiety. This is the part of the brain that is responsible for storing memories of threatening events in your life. It appears smaller in people who have experienced such events as childhood abuse or served in combat.

Hypothalamus - This is the command center of the brain. It communicates the fight or flight response.

Factors that can increase your risk for anxiety:

- **Stress** - excessive or unresolved stress in your life.
- **Genetics** - if someone in your family has anxiety, then you may also suffer from it.
- **Trauma** - if you have suffered a severe trauma, someone close to you has suffered a severe trauma, or you have witnessed a severe trauma.

- **Gender** - sadly, the reality is that women suffer from anxiety more than men.

The other part of the anxiety that gets talked about is triggers or a triggering event, anything that induces a fight or flight feeling, in some the brain basically shuts down and now we're only thinking with our 'lizard' brain, not thinking rationally. In psychology, a trigger is a stimulus from one of the five senses - smell, sound, sight, taste or touch - that causes a trigger of feelings to a past trauma. It can also be classified as post-traumatic stress disorder (PTSD).

Triggers are personal and different for everyone, so there isn't a one size fits all fix. It is impossible to avoid triggers but learning to manage them is possible with help. Whether a trained therapist or life coach, understanding the underlying issues you can work on coping mechanisms such as meditation, tapping (EFT), and breathwork.

Triggers can show up as a sense of déjà vu, and it's possible you don't even know you're being triggered until you're in the middle of it.

Some events or situations that can cause you to be triggered:

- Someone resembling your abuser or has similar traits as them.
- Even having to interact with your abuser because maybe you share a child together.

- A place or situation where something occurred that was traumatic.
- Sounds of anger, pain, or fear.
- Smells that remind you of a time when you were abused or witnessed something traumatic.

In my case, I became a mute; I had an extremely hard time trying to communicate, I couldn't form proper sentences and all I knew was that I had to encourage myself. There was a feeling of butterflies or nausea in the pit of my stomach, and then depending on the level of stress or severity of the trigger, I would start to sweat or shake. Then I would go straight into predicting the future or catastrophizing the situation, and nothing would bring my brain back to anything positive.

Now it must be said that if you experience any of these once in a while that is a perfectly normal part of life. There will always be something that makes you a little anxious or apprehensive, and it can make us motivated to act. But if these occurrences happen regularly over a period of six months or more and you have tried some of the techniques I have presented below to try to mitigate some of your overthinking and anxiety with little success, then I strongly urge you to seek medical treatment from a professional This is a treatable disease/disorder, but without proper care it can become worse over time and sometimes even fatal.

Destructive Thinking

We all have struggles and go through hard times. But it's what we do with those hard times that can help or hinder our way of thinking. It can be hard to feel good and think negatively when it feels like the world is stacked against you. Life is rarely perfect, nor is it as awful as our brains may have us think it is.

Below are some of the ways that we sabotage our joy and happiness and add to our stress and tendency to overthink.

- **Predicting the Future**: This is when your mind takes any problem or situation that crosses your path and just *knows* how it's going to pan out. You can see with full clarity how the issue is going to resolve, usually with bad results. You have your weekly touch-base with your boss coming up, and you just know they are going to bring up that project you messed up the week before. There is no way around it, they will point out all the things you did wrong because you feel like lately you've been messing things up a lot. You consider calling in sick the day of your meeting because you don't want to hear about how you screwed up the project, and the thought makes you almost vomit from nerves.

- **Focusing on the Negatives**: This is when your mind only focuses on the negative, there is no room for positive. In any given situation, all that is seen is the negative aspects. In fact, you tend to forget any mentions of anything positive that anyone has ever said to you. You decide to wear a new outfit to work and a few people compliment you on the outfit, but for some reason, you don't like the way the top fits, and so you think they're just being nice, there's no way they can mean it. Can't they see how it's really too tight and shows all your fat? What made you think you could pull off this look? And to top it all off, your hair is all wrong today and the shoes just don't work.

- **Comparing or Envy**: I like to call this 'comparysis.' Nowadays, in the age of social media and everyone appearing to put their best foot forward and having highly curated accounts, it's easy to get caught up in all the "Why isn't my life like that?" It's easy to start comparing all the things the Joneses have and you don't. The brain starts to focus on all the negative aspects of your life in relation to theirs, then the jealousy starts, and you feel miserable.

- **Personalizing & Blaming**: This is when you will generally blame yourself for everything. You can't do anything right, even when there is no evidence that it was, in fact, your fault. The flip side is that you always blame others for everything even when there is evidence that you are at fault. Similar to finger-pointing, it is always someone else's fault.

- **Catastrophizing**: This is when your mind looks at a situation and blows it so far out of proportion that no matter how it ends it will be a catastrophe.

- **Ruminating**: What if? Did I say the wrong thing? You find yourself going over and over and over the same thing in your head and no matter what you do, you can't seem to let the subject go. This is usually something that has happened in the past; it could last night, a week ago or even a few years ago, you are still thinking about it and you are exhausted, physically and emotionally.

- **All-or-nothing**: Anything less than perfection will do; anything less than that is seen as failure. Everything has to be a complete success, or you may as well crawl under a rock and die.

- **Over-generalizations**: Something happens to you once and then you paint everything that comes after with a broad brushstroke. That is how everything is going to happen.

- **Mind reading**: Projecting thoughts and feelings onto others. Everything thinks you're a loser. Assuming that people think poorly of you, even when there is no evidence to support this.

- **Magnification and Minimization**: You have a tendency to make a mountain of a molehill, and small blunders are blown *way* out of proportion or you completely disregard something big that you did.
- **Should'ing**: "I should do this." "I should do that." This is a totally useless vocabulary, and it is not just demotivating but also makes you feel guilty for not doing the things that you think you should be doing.

Noticing the types of destructive thinking you gravitate too will go a long way to destroying the nasty little buggers. But they can be subtle so recognizing them can take time and a lot of introspection.

When do you find them surfacing? What types of situations or what relationships do you currently engage with?

A few years ago, my friend Jennifer was in a very bad position. She had just left an emotionally abusive relationship but still had to deal with her ex due to them having a child together. Obviously, she had to see this person due to visitations, but the exchanges were so difficult as they´ve been constantly triggered. Every time during the exchanges, they became verbally abusive that she had to have someone companying her all the time. She was never able to form a thought and when she did, all she could think of was having to defend her position, which angered the other party even more. Even having to discuss the situation with the Powers That Be (judges, lawyers, counselors, mediators, etc.) was extremely difficult. Partway through a discussion, she would usually burst into tears out of frustration for not being able to explain. After walking away from these encounters, she would always ruminate over what she didn't say or what she should have said. Then she would start catastrophizing the situation, and her brain would go round and round and round in circles, always with the absolute worst-case scenarios she could think of happening. No matter what she´s been told about the situation, she just couldn't stop myself. Not only that, but I couldn't stop talking about it with anyone who would listen. She would rehash old news over and over. It was exhausting.

It took a lot of inner work and really working on changing the thought patterns and seeing them for what they were, fight or flight instincts that were no longer serving Jen. It is hard work, but the peace of mind that comes at the end of the long, dark tunnel is worth it. Now Jen is able to see her ex, chat briefly, even sit across a table from them and discuss visitations (with a judge present) without a lawyer as her buffer.

To change these thought patterns, you must challenge them. To do that you need to more intentional with your thinking, which will be covered in a later chapter.

Part 2: Practice

"Only I can change my life; no one else can do it for me."

~Carol Burnett~

Chapter 5: How to Stop Overthinking?

"You don't have to see the whole staircase, just take the first step."

- Martin Luther King

The best way to start controlling the overthinking is simply awareness. Start to be aware of what's happening and recognize when you are in the midst of a downward spiral pattern. Granted, it can be hard to see the forest for the trees when you are in the thick of a panic attack or so angry, that you can't see straight, but starting to see the patterns and when you are being triggered is the first step to combating it. Try to step back to look objectively at the situation and how you are responding to it. This is planting the seed of change. It will take time, but with patience, time and giving yourself the grace to mess up from time to time, you will soon learn to manage your thoughts.

You may not even recognize the pattern until a day or two later or even a week but congratulate yourself that you are now able to start seeing those patterns and what is happening. Don't beat yourself up over it. Acknowledge it, maybe journal on it. This is where meditation, breathwork, visualizations, tapping (EFT–Emotional Freedom Tapping) and/or NLP (Neuro-linguistic Programming) can come in handy.

Only give thought to what can go right. Overthinking is generally caused by one single emotion: fear. When you think about all the things that can go wrong or might happen in the future, it's easy to become paralyzed and just not do anything. The next time you sense that you are starting to spiral downward, stop! Instead, visualize all that can go right, and keep those thoughts at the forefront of your thoughts that day. Try to distract yourself. When you find yourself getting caught up in a downward loop of black thoughts, find a way to distract yourself with happy, positive alternatives - meditation, yoga, dancing, a walk in the nature, anything that you enjoy doing and will do because you enjoy them, not something you do because you think it will help. You must find something that truly lights you up, or you won't continue doing it in the long term. These things can help distance you from the issues long enough to stop the overthinking.

Give yourself some perspective. The brain always likes making things seem bigger and more negative than they really are. So the next time you catch yourself trying to make a mountain out of a molehill, ask yourself will whatever you're worrying about even matter in a year? How about in six months? Heck! Will it matter a week from now? Asking this simple question can sometimes shut down the overthinking in its tracks.

Change how you view your fears. Remember that failing in the past or making mistakes doesn't mean you should fear trying. Just because something didn't work once, doesn't mean it will always be that way. Remember, every opportunity is a chance to try again.

Put a timer on for your brain. Give yourself a boundary, set a timer for a period when you are allowed to worry, mull over, fret, and analyze the situation. Give yourself five minutes, 10 minutes whatever is reasonable for you, but once the timer goes off you should write down everything that is/was worrying you, stressing you out, or giving you anxiety. Set a timer again for this piece. When the timer goes off, rip up the piece of paper, burn it or throw it out and then move on.

Understand that you can't predict the future. Spend your time in the present. When you worry about the future or the past, you rob yourself of enjoying what's right in front of you. What's happening *now*! Focusing on the future is simply not productive because you have no control over what will happen; focus on the here and now and on the things that bring you joy.

Learn to accept that you are good enough. This is something maximizers will struggle with because it is one of our greatest fears, that we aren't good enough or worthy enough. This fear is what our overthinking is often rooted in. If you've tried your best, whether you failed or succeeded, accept it and know that you've done all that you possibly could.

Be grateful. It is physically impossible to be resentful and grateful at the same time, so why not focus on the positive things?

One last thing to consider when you feel the need to overthink, instead of analyzing each and every angle of the problem, what if you went on your gut instinct? In times of crisis, we tend to forget that our body and our brain 'knows' what to do because we are so busy trying to be rational and right. Go with what feels right, if possible. As humans, we amass a slew of information on a daily basis and through our work, in some instances, we have become experts in our field, so why not trust that somewhere deep in the recesses of your mind you "know" the answer.

Summary to master the awareness:

- Notice when you're stuck in your head, keep the focus on problem-solving.
- Calm down anxiety.
- Breathe, and admit that you're anxious or angry. Challenge your thoughts, release anxiety or anger. Visualize yourself calm, think it through. Listen to music. Change your focus.

Visualization

Visualization is one of the best ways to get your brain back on track when you find yourself getting off balance. Try listening to slow, calm music or try visualizing your day, as this can help you mentally prepare for whatever comes up because 'stuff' will always happen.

Visualizing is mental imagery used to imagine a best-case scenario. It requires you to want something, perceive it, feel it, and then believe in it - that it is yours. Believing you have something before it manifests can alter the mind in profound ways. It prepares your subconscious to believe you already have what you seek, which, in turn, causes a boost in confidence.

Our brains have a hard time telling the difference between reality and imagination, even if you don't have a calm mind but you can visualize what that would look and feel like *and* believe it wholeheartedly, the brain will do what it can to make that your reality.

Now believing you have one million dollars when you're struggling to put food on the table will be a little hard to imagine, and the brain will have some difficulties with this. But if you imagine that you have an extra $100 left between paydays so that putting food on the table isn't so difficult, then the brain can grasp that and help you find ways to manifest that money.

Some ways to do this are:

- Motivational visualization - imagine your end goal and the feelings that will come from accomplishing that goal. Immerse yourself in it, feel it, believe it, then your motivation to reach that success will become more realistic.

- Define what you want - learn to turn your focus away from the negative, from what you don't want to the things that you do want. The more detailed visualization and goal you can imagine the better for the brain it will be.

Visualization is the best tool for the Law of Attraction. When you treat your world and the universe like your own personal supermarket, then that's when things will really start to fall into place.

Try manifesting something small to start, something that you would like but have no real attachment to. It would be nice to have but won't be the end of the world if you don't receive it. Sit and think about it for a few minutes. How will receiving this thing feel? Can you touch it? Can you see it clearly? Focus on the feelings that arise when you see it in your mind's eye. The universe responds best to feelings. Once you have a clear picture of this thing and the feelings associated with it, then the hard part is to release it to the universe. What I mean by this is, simply give the universe thanks for working to send you this thing and then don't think about it anymore. If you focus on it and think about it too much, then the energy you put out is one of desperation and lack and will put up resistance to it coming to you. If you cannot think about it at all, then the energy behind it is one of abundance, and there is no resistance to bring it to you. The universe responds to abundance.

Breathwork

Now, I'm not talking about the type of breathwork that requires a properly trained practitioner, although is that is something that you can consider. What I am talking about is just taking a few minutes out of your day when you feel an anxiety attack coming on or feel your brain start to go down it's dark path of negative thoughts, stop for a moment and place one hand on your heart and one your stomach and consciously change your pattern of breathing for a few moments. Breathe deeper, and count while breathing. Breath in for a count of four, hold for a count of five, and breath out for a count of six. Consciously changing our pattern of breathing can promote a sense of calm and deep relaxation; it helps to decrease our levels of stress.

Breathwork has been known to improve mental, physical, and spiritual well-being and can assist with enriching your creativity, increasing joy, reducing stress and anxiety, releasing negative thoughts, and aid in positive personal development.

But to get started you can always try YouTube for some beginner training on breathwork and decide from there if it's something that you would like to explore more in-depth with a certified, trained practitioner.

Emotional Freedom Technique (EFT or tapping)

Emotional Freedom Technique or so-called Tapping provides relief from emotional issues, PTSD, disorders and physical diseases to name a few.

While this type of 'medicine' is fairly new to North American culture, the concepts behind it have been in practice in Eastern medicine for over 5000 years.

Similar to Acupressure and Acupuncture, EFT uses meridian points on the body to stimulate energy by tapping them with your fingertips, using your own energy to heal your body. We are composed of energy and if one part of that (emotional) is disrupted then it can affect the whole (physical) part. You cannot treat one without the other. Restoring one will restore the other. Restoring this balance helps to keep the body and mind in balance, which, in turn, will fight off any diseases or sicknesses.

Tapping simply focuses on a negative feeling or emotion or problem that is bothering you, and while concentrating on that issue, you use your fingers to tap on each of the nine meridian points. While tapping these points, you concentrate on accepting and resolving the negative emotion.

When you start tapping, use a firm but gentle pressure, kind of like tapping a desk. You can use all four fingers or just the index and middle finger. I prefer to use just the two, especially for the more sensitive areas around the eyes.

Meridian points:

- Hand (Karate Chop) - using four fingers tap the side of the hand opposite the thumb
- Eyebrow - Inner edge by the bridge of the nose
- Side of eye - Hard area between the eye and the temple
- Under the eye - Hard area directly below the eye
- Under nose - Just above the upper lip
- Chin - Directly below the nose meridian, about halfway between the lower lip and the chin
- Collarbone - Just below the ridge of your collarbone and just to the left or right of the horseshoe indent
- Underarm - Approximately four inches below your armpit (around the bra strap area for women)
- Top of head - The crown of your head

Now before you get started with your tapping, you need to set a marker for how you are feeling. I like to place my hands on my heart, close my eyes for a moment, and feel into the emotion and decide on a scale of 1-10 how I am feeling about the issue or problem at hand. Ideally, whatever the number is, when I am done tapping, I want it to be below five, usually I like to be around two or three. If I'm not, then I start the tapping sequence over again.

Once you are ready to start, you want to have a setup statement ready.

"Even though I feel this anxiety, I deeply and completely accept myself.

Even though I feel exhausted and unclear, I fully love and honor myself.

Even though I'm feeling anxious about my finances, I deeply and completely love myself."

With your four fingers, start tapping the Karate Chop point on your hand while repeating this setup statement three times. Now you're ready to move on to the next point.

Here is a sample script you can modify as you need for your given situation.

While tapping on the karate chop:

"Even though I feel anxious and exhausted, I fully love and
accept myself.

Even though I feel anxious and exhausted, I fully love and
accept myself.

Even though I feel anxious and exhausted, I fully love and
accept myself."

Round 1

Eyebrow: I feel so anxious

Side of eye: I am so tired

Under eye: I feel lost

Under nose: I have a total lack of clarity

Chin: This creates fear inside of me

Collarbone: This makes me feel more anxious

Underarm: This makes me feel more tired

Top of head: This makes me feel more afraid

Round 2

Eyebrow: I want to release these feelings

Side of eye: I want to feel at peace

Under eye: I want to feel free and alert

Under nose: I want to feel certain

Chin: I want to feel energized

Collarbone: I want to feel a sense of ease

Underarm: I want to feel safe

Top of head: I want to feel connected to the universe

Round 3:

Eyebrow: I allow myself to release this

Side of eye: I allow myself to feel at peace

Under eye: I allow myself to feel free

Under nose: I allow myself to be certain

Chin: I allow to be energized

Collarbone: I allow this all with ease

Underarm: I allow myself to feel safe

Top of head: I allow myself to connect with the universe

Round 4:

Eyebrow: I love releasing what is no longer serving me

Side of eye: I love settling into peace

Under eye: I love feeling free

Under nose: I love being certain

Chin: I love being full of life force energy

Collarbone: I love feeling safe

Underarm: I love that this all comes to me easily

Top of head: I love that I am connected deeply with the universe

Round 5:

Eyebrow: Thank you, universe, for supporting me fully.

Side of eye: Thank you, universe, for granting me peace.

Under eye: Thank you, universe, for showing me feeling free.

Under nose: Thank you, universe, for giving me certainty.

Chin: Thank you, universe, for infusing me with energy.

Collarbone: Thank you, universe, for keeping me safe.

Underarm: Thank you, universe, for giving this all to me with ease.

Top of head: Thank you, universe, for connecting with me and supporting me fully whenever I ask.

Once you have completed the five rounds, go back to placing your hands on your heart and see how you feel now. Has your original number gone down? How far down? Don't feel that you have failed if your number has only dropped one or two points. That's a start. It can take time for the energy to even out. Go back and repeat the script again until you feel able to relax and the number has dropped below a five.

Also, consider changing up the script a bit to account for the work you are trying to do to correct the anxiety or fear or whatever emotion it is. "Even though I have some remaining anxiety, I completely and deeply accept myself," or "Even though I'm still fearful about the problem, I deeply love and honor myself." Then continue with the tapping sequence as above, until you feel in control and your number is lower.

When EFT will not work is when you stop making the issue about you. Let's say you just found out your grandmother is very sick. This upsets you to the point of not being able to focus on anything but her health. So, you decide to try some tapping. You cannot say "Even though my grandmother is sick, I deeply and completely accept myself." This is not putting the focus on your issue. What you should say is, "Even though I'm sad my grandmother is sick, I deeply and completely accept myself." Do you see the difference?

While there have been many success stories using this technique, it still isn't completely understood by the medical community. That's not to say that it doesn't work. I have had some success in reducing my anxiety due to various issues. But that's not to say that it will work for you. EFT is just one of many options to assist with maintaining anxiety, fear, and analysis paralysis due to overthinking. Give it a try and see, but maintain the practice for a week or two before deciding if it works. As with anything it takes practice and consistency.

Neuro-linguistic Programming (NLP)

Neuro-linguistic Programming is about understanding the neurology and language of the brain. The neuro stands for neurology - particularly how states of mind and body affect communication and behaviors, linguistic stands for the language of the brain-mind and body states are revealed in our language and non-verbal communication, and programming refers to the capacity to change our mind and body states, our neuro language functions.

You have a conscious and unconscious mind, the conscious mind is thought to be the goal-setter, and the unconscious mind is thought to be the goal-getter. You consciously set goals for yourself and then your unconscious mind will do what it can to bring them to fruition, but if the two aren't speaking the same language then the unconscious brain will bring you what it thinks you need, not necessarily what you thought about or asked it to bring you.

Have you ever heard someone say or have you ever said that you feel like you're living on autopilot? This is thought to be living based on your own programming; the beliefs, traditions, thoughts, etc. that have shaped you. Through NLP you can learn, or unlearn, to change these autopilot behaviors.

Based on this, NLP uses perceptual, behavioral, and communication techniques to make it easier for you to change your thoughts and actions.

You need to be clear with what you're asking for in order for your unconscious mind to get it. Think of it like a menu. You're in a foreign country and decide to get something to eat, you think you're ordered a steak but in reality, you ordered frogs legs. You did not get what you visualized. The same can be said for your life, if you're ordering more money, a better job, or happy, healthy relationships but none of that is what is showing up in your life, then something is getting lost in translation.

What is happening is that your unconscious mind is giving you what it thinks you really want. NLP is the user manual for your brain. It is intended to help improve your self-awareness, communication skills, and confidence. It helps you understand your own mind, how you came to think and behave the way you do, to manage your moods and emotions, and to help reprogram how you process information.

There is a lot online about NLP, again YouTube is a great source of information, but you can also consider certified practitioners to help you understand it at a greater depth.

Chapter 6: Intentional Thinking

"Take time to deliberate, but when the time for action has arrived, stop thinking and go in."

- Napoleon Bonaparte

T he brain has something called neuroplasticity, and it has been shown that the pathways between the amygdala and hippocampus can get severely damaged with constant exposure to stress but because of neuroplasticity, these patterns don't have to remain permanent.

The brain and the body can recover; however, the younger you are the easier it is to create new neural pathways. That is not to say that as you age you can't create these new pathways; it just becomes a little more difficult.

There are activities that can combat stress and wear and tear on the brain, regardless of your age. Such as exercise, meditation, and socializing - not cutting yourself off from the outside world.

As stated in an earlier chapter, there are tenants living rent-free in your brain and I provided some tips to evict them.

Once you have identified the tenants and started the process to evict them, the next step is to identify the mental tapes of movies that these tenants start to play. You have probably become aware of just how negative these movies and stories really are. It won't matter if you've had five or six successes, they will focus on the one time you messed something up or did something wrong. Once you've identified it, write it down. The act of putting pen to paper clears it from your head.

This is also a trick I like to use at nighttime when my brain won't shut off. Every last thing I've been thinking about during the day or even if an old issue rears its ugly head, I write that down too. Once I've brain dumped everything, I am able to fall back asleep. This a way of disassociating with the issue, writing it down makes it seem less important than when it was rattling around in your head. You are able to distance yourself from the feelings behind it.

Now find the lie. Somewhere along the way, we chose to believe something about ourselves that most likely isn't true. Maybe, back then in school, you told yourself you were dumb because you were having difficulty grasping some math equation. Maybe someone said you were worthless or a nobody. Whatever it is, write it down next to the mental tape or movie you have written down.

This is where intentional thinking really comes into play. You now need to replace the lie with the truth. This can be much easier said than done sometimes, but it's the only way to combat these destructive thoughts. Reflect, pray or meditate, now would be a good time to sit in stillness for a while and be guided to the answer.

When the answer comes to you write it down next to the lie and the mental tape story. Whatever comes to you, write it in as positive a form as you can. Instead of "I am not worthless," write "I am worthy of all the success I have accomplished in my career."

Weeding out the truths and lies and evicting your destructive tenants will go far to mastering and controlling your mind and its thoughts.

You will really need to challenge all your old thoughts and paradigms about yourself and what these tenants have been telling you for years. It won't be easy, but the end result will be worth it. Be consistent and diligent. Don't let them continue to live rent-free.

Shifting Paradigms

To really become intentional with your thinking you need to start recognizing and challenging your old thought patterns and paradigms that have been your reality for so long.

Learning to catch yourself thinking these thoughts will be one step in many to help stop your overthinking patterns. Also noticing the feelings and emotions that precipitate these patterns will help to interrupt them.

Noticing just what you are thinking is another tool. Once you can start observing your patterns and correct them then you are on your way. When you catch yourself thinking you're a "bad parent," why not try and switch it up to "I notice that I'm thinking I'm a bad parent." If you are able, try taking it a step further and see if you can't find a truth that supports being a bad parent. I bet you can't find one.

Consider setting a deadline. Overthinking is like a paragraph with no grammar, it just goes on and on and on with no end in sight. That serves no one and makes it difficult to know when you have reached a conclusion or a solution to your problem. Why not set a deadline for the thought? Tell yourself gently that you have another 10 minutes to 'worry' about the problem and try to come up with a solution. If not, then you are moving on to other things.

Listening to music can help distract the brain from its worrisome thoughts. It's like your overactive brain can't keep thinking its thoughts when you're distracting it with music you really like and dancing around the house. Pick a theme song that you plugin every time your brain is going into overdrive over some issue.

Shock your brain into thinking about other things. If your brain won't shut off, consider dropping and doing 10 push-ups, or how about smelling a scent you really like, maybe lavender oil or some flowers, or sticking your hand into some cold water. The point here is to shock your brain into thinking "Wow, those flowers smell really nice," or "Holy cow, that's some cold water!" This gives the brain something else to worry about for a time.

Dump the perfectionism. Overthinking and perfectionism can go hand in hand just as overthinking and procrastination. You need to push yourself to try even if mistakes will be made. Mistakes are where the magic happens. Don't give up on something or not even try just because you think you won't be any good or you won't ace it the first time. Make mistakes, regret those mistakes, and then move on.

Mastering Your Thoughts

Mastering anything takes time, dedication, focus, consistency, and positive forward action. Mastering your thoughts and mindset is no different. In fact, this is probably the most important thing to master if you wish to have a prosperous, calm, and happy life.

Some ways to start mastering your mindset are:

- **Check your cup** - Are you filling up your cup every chance you get? Are you making sure that you recharge yourself? We can't keep putting others first and expect ourselves to be operating at our best. If we are always putting others' needs ahead of our own, it's no wonder you are tired and getting short and sharp with friends and family. Putting your needs ahead of others is not selfish, it's vital.

- **Word check** - Notice the words you use every day about yourself and about others. Are they positive or negative? Do you tell yourself "I am" and "I can" or "I won't" and "I can't?" How you speak to yourself will have a huge impact on your mindset.

- **Inspirational tribe** - Who do you spend your time with? We are the sum of the five people we associate with the most. Who is in your circle? Do they lift you up or drag you down? Really look at where you are spending your time and with whom.

Decision Making

As mentioned in an earlier chapter, we know that willpower and productivity diminish over the course of a day.

So, to end analysis paralysis and take back the power of your thoughts and become more intentional with your decision-making, try these suggestions below:

Structure your day for decision-making - not all decisions are created equal. Choosing what kind of toothpaste to buy is not nearly as important as what school to send your kids too (public or private), so structure your day to tackle more important decisions in the morning when your willpower is at its peak. Try to keep the afternoon free for smaller, less important decisions. This is when meal planning would come in handy, that way when you get home from work you know exactly what is for dinner as opposed to grabbing take out or having junk food because you are too tired to cook.

Intentionally limit the amount of information you consume - determine what you're researching or willing to learn, then read only for that specific purpose. Determine how many sources of information you may need for this, then stick to that limit.

Intentionally set a time limit - not only should you limit the amount of information you consume but you need to consider setting a time limit as well. It's too easy to get caught in old patterns of mindlessly scrolling through pages and pages of websites, not really working on the task at hand. It has been proven that work expands to fill the time allotted for it, so by limiting the amount of time you have to make a decision you are forced to make a decision quickly. While this is a self-imposed deadline and you may have a hard time following it or even believing that the deadline is real, consider making the deadline public. By that, I mean to tell someone who you trust and who will hold you accountable.

Chapter 7: Positive Self-Talk

T he practice of positive self-talk is one of the fastest ways to get out of your head. It is the practice of being optimistic and seeing the positive in just about any situation. When you can't see the positive, you are at least aware of the situation enough that it doesn't send you into a tailspin of negative thinking. You are able to see the situation for what it is.

By now, I hope you have been able to identify some of the ways that you are sabotaging your mental health and are now becoming more aware of when it occurs. Now it won't be easy to turn the negative self-talk around, but with some diligence and consistency, it is possible. It requires practice, time, and some grace toward yourself when you slip up.

What is Self-Talk?

Self-talk is the internal chatter, your internal dialogue that goes on between yourself and your brain. It's this internal chatter that can be both positive and negative, it can be encouraging, or it can be distressing, and this can largely depend on your personality. If you are an optimist, then your inner dialogue will be more positive, which offers some health benefits and a better quality of life. The opposite can be said of being a pessimist, but with diligence and hard work, the negative self-talk can be turned around regardless of your personality and upbringing.

Positive self-talk has many benefits, including enhancing your general well-being, increasing your physical well-being and less stress. Other health benefits can include:

- Increased vitality
- Greater life satisfaction
- Better immune system
- Pain relief

No one really knows why this works and why people with a more positive outlook on life experience these benefits, but research suggests that these people may have the mental skills to be able to cope with stressful situations, which can reduce the harmful effects of stress.

Louise Hay, the well-known author of *Heal Your Life and Heal Your Body*, put this into practice when she was diagnosed with cervical cancer in 1978. She considered alternative options to surgery and instead decided to put together her own intensive program. Using affirmations, visualizations, nutritional cleansing, and psychotherapy she was able to cure her cancer completely within six months.

How to Practice

It will take time to catch the negative self-talk because it's become so ingrained in you and feels so normal, but it can be changed with practice. Once you start to recognize your patterns, then you can start to address the best practices for you.

Examples:

Negative: I failed, why did I even try? Now I'm embarrassed.

Positive: Wow! I'm proud of myself for trying something new. That was brave of me.

Negative: I've never done this before, why did I even try, I'll be so bad at it.

Positive: This is a great opportunity for me to learn something new.

Mirror talk - this may seem silly and feel awkward at first but talk to yourself in the mirror. Look yourself in the eyes and talk. Tell yourself you love yourself, that you love your hair, your eyes, whatever it is, just start talking positively to yourself about yourself.

Affirmations - write affirmations everywhere around your house. On your door as you leave the house, in kitchen drawers, on your bathroom mirror, in the car, etc. Seeing and reading these affirmations will have a positive effect on your brain and boost your serotonin, which is the 'happy' chemical in our brains because it promotes happiness and well-being.

Positive people - look at who you are surrounding yourself with, whether you believe it or not we feed off the energy of those we associate with, so find people that inspire you, lift you up, and cheer you on.

Gratitude

Given all the ideas listed throughout this book, I felt this one deserves its own heading as I strongly believe it is one of the fastest ways to turn negative self-talk into positive and set yourself up for success.

Gratitude is defined as an overall sense of feeling grateful. An emotion expressing appreciation for what you have.

It can exist as both a temporary feeling and an inherent part of who you are. Gratitude requires a recognition of something occurring that was positive and outside of you. While most of this book has been directed at healing our inner world and that is crucial to sorting through overthinking and our anxiety and depression, we also need to accept that some external forces are necessary to make us happy, but we need to show gratitude for these things.

It is generally seen as a spontaneous feeling, but it is also increasingly becoming a part of a practice to count your blessings and be grateful for what's in front of and around you. Because of this, you can deliberately cultivate a feeling of gratitude.

Gratitude Matters

It is possible to feel grateful for loved ones, colleagues, and life in general. This emotion generates an atmosphere of positivity. You will find that over time, this feeling boost happiness and promotes physical and emotional health, even when struggling with mental health obstacles. It may be a little harder to dig for the gratitude in such instances, but with practice, time and consistency you will find it is your go-to for tough times.

Practicing gratitude curbs the negative words and thoughts, and it shifts your inner attention away from anger, resentment, and jealousy, which minimizes the possibility of spiraling downward into ruminating or catastrophizing the situation.

Gratitude starts with noticing the goodness in your life, which can be hard in this world of materialism and constant comparing to others via social media, but it is possible.

It can start small, just noticing something in your day that you are grateful for, maybe it's your job because that allows you to put food on your table, or your house and having a roof over your head so you are safe, maybe it's your car because the crowding on transit makes you uncomfortable. Whatever it is, be thankful, be grateful and show it, acknowledge it. I keep a journal and write in it every morning and/or evening at least three to five things that I am grateful for that day. It has made such a difference in how I view things and react to things.

Gratitude is by far the biggest tool that has seen me through some dark days. Being able to be grateful for any given situation knowing that it is for my highest good has turned most of my negative self-talk and dark thought spirals around to positive. When I catch myself slipping back into a negative frame of mind, all I have to do is quickly list off a few things I'm grateful for and the negativity melts away.

It wasn't always like this; it took time, practice, and consistency.

Now the real magic in gratitude that I have discovered happens when you are able to start being grateful for the people and issues in your life that challenge you. For example, you've just gone through a horrible divorce and custody battle for your children. You loathe your ex for all that he/she has put you through, but without this person, you wouldn't have your amazing kids. So, you realize that you are grateful to him/her for giving you such a gift. Now, I realize this may sound a little farfetched and hard to fathom, but I can speak from experience that this does work. I have recently gone through this very thing. While I am not a fan of my ex at all, I am extremely grateful for the gift of my child who wouldn't be in this world without my ex. Believe it or not, shifting to this way of thinking has made the court trips and such a little easier to deal with.

If that seems a little difficult in the beginning, then try this:

- Who has inspired you? Why?
- Keep a gratitude journal - Write big and little joys of daily life or try and identify three to five good things that happened that day.
- Try to imagine what your life would look like if some particular positive even hadn't happened.

Chapter 8: Mindfulness

"You can't always control what goes on outside, but you can always control what goes on inside."

- Wayne Dyer

W hen struggling with overthinking, anxiety, depression or any kind of fear-based issues, it can be hard to contemplate something even resembling mindfulness. Our brains are very good at trying to take care of us and trying to keep us safe, but in keeping us safe, it also tends to keep us stuck in reliving the past or trying to predict the future, which keeps us stuck and unable to just enjoy life and all the wonderful things it has to offer.

Instead of focusing on the negative and the anxiety, start to think the thoughts you really want to think, start by asking yourself, how do I want to feel? Is this something I want to be thinking about? Do I want to be worried about it? When the answer comes to you, then ask yourself, what would I be thinking, if I wasn't thinking about the negative? How would it feel to be thinking right?

What you will find is that when you are being more mindful of your thoughts and starting to focus on more positive thoughts and feelings, your brain will automatically start tapping to that feeling. Now, this may not happen right away; it may take time because right now your brain is wired to automatically think negative, fearful thoughts so it may push back a bit, to begin with. But stick with it.

Once you start to get a handle on the things you want to think about, it's time to start envisioning the person you want to be. Are you looking to banish your anxiety and fears? Then start to envision a person who is confident and take charge, who knows what they want and isn't afraid to ask for it. What would this person's day look like? Who do they interact with? How do they deal with difficulties during their day? How do they spend their time? Map out what a day in the life would like and feel like, this gives your brain something to focus on and work toward.

Next, you have to decide. Is this something you are committed to doing? So many times, people have the best of intentions when starting new habits, but sticking them out, in the long run, can be hard. Create your own "why." Having a "why", that desires for something, is what will help you on those long nights when your brain decides "Nope, we're going to go over that discussion you had with your boss when you said it."

This is when you return to your why of not thinking negative thoughts anymore and tell your brain that you are done thinking these thoughts. It happened, I'm not rehashing it over and over.

What is Mindfulness?

Mindfulness. Such a simple word. Yet packed with so much meaning. Mindfulness can simply be defined as the practice of paying attention to the present moment. It is the intentional practice of observing one's thoughts and actions and accepting things, in a non-judgmental manner, one's thoughts and behaviors are neither good nor bad, they just are.

You learn to bring your attention to the experiences occurring in the present moment without any judgment. Being fully present, aware of where we are, and what we are doing. By being fully present you are unable to rehash the past or focus on what might be coming in the future.

Mindfulness is about being aware of time. However, everyone's definition of time can be different, especially when fears and insecurities about the past or the future raise their ugly heads, which can then make it difficult to be mindful and appreciate the present.

This is something that every human being has access to, we already possess the ability to be mindful, but so often we veer off course due to our overly scheduled lives. While this state is innate in all of us, it is something that, in this day and age of hustle and bustle and material wants and desires, needs to be cultivated.

Mindfulness is critical in that it helps people accept their life experiences, including that bad ones we would rather forget, rather than reacting to those experiences with aversion or avoidance. It helps us to accept that these experiences are now a part of our makeup and who we are. There is little point in ruminating over what might have been and just accept in a non-judgmental way that these experiences were. But they are no more.

Benefits of Mindfulness

There are many benefits to being mindful.

Improved well-being - being mindful makes it easier to appreciate the little things in life. Savor pleasures as they occur. Be better able to manage adverse events in your life when they occur. You are better able to deep, lasting connections with others.

Improves physical well-being - if having a clear mind and appreciating life isn't enough, then maybe having better physical health will tempt you. It can assist with lowering blood pressure, improve your sleep, and help reduce stress.

I firmly believe the benefits of being mindful is simply being able to be more present in whatever situation comes your way. You will find yourself being able to be more playful and truly enjoying time with your kids. You will be able to enjoy more long meaningful conversations with family and friends because you won't be distracted by your phone or thoughts of past and future issues. You will also be able to unwind at the end of the day easier and therefore have better nights sleeps.

Once you start practicing mindfulness on a regular basis, you will most likely find yourself feeling calmer, happier, more patient, and generally better able to handle issues and transitions that occur throughout your day.

To live mindfully is to live fully in the present moment rather than dwelling on the past or attempting to anticipate the future. Being mindful also means being aware of your emotions and when they aren't serving you. I'm not saying it's okay to stuff them down and ignore them; that does no good, but neither does being ruled by them. Mindfulness allows us to acknowledge our feelings/emotions without judgment and work through them.

Getting started

Learn to set aside time - you don't need anything special, like a meditation bench or cushion, to practice mindfulness but you do need to set aside some time and some space to work on it.

Observe the present moment as it is - the idea behind mindfulness is not necessarily to quiet the mind or achieve some state of calm. It's more about acknowledging what is going on in your world, inner and outer, and just being aware of the present moment, without judgment, regardless of what is happening. I do realize this is probably easier said than done, but it is a crucial piece to mindfulness.

Let judgments roll on by - when you see the judgments rise, all you want to do is acknowledge them, make a mental note of them, and move on. Don't dwell on them.

Return to observing the present moment - while practicing mindfulness, you will find your mind wanders and gets hung up on various thoughts. This is why mindfulness is a practice about returning again and again to the present moment.

Be kind to your wandering mind - be kind to yourself when you catch your mind wandering. It may pick up a stray thought and try to get you to focus and dwell on it. Don't judge yourself for this will happen, just recognize what has happened and gently bring your mind back to the present moment.

Sit by yourself, be aware of your breath and the sounds around you. Focus on each breath and the sensations of the chair supporting you, the temperature, and anything else that comes to mind.

Once you have settled into a rhythm with your breathing, you can then shift your attention to the thoughts and emotions you are experiencing. Do not judge these thoughts and feelings, just acknowledge them and then let them go, like clouds on a breeze. If this elicits some form of an emotional reaction, then explore that reaction, but again, with no judgment.

At this point, you may want to journal your thoughts and feelings and your reactions to these. You don't have to explore them right away, but some freewriting can unearth long-held feelings and thoughts that you didn't even know were there that could explain why you reacted the way you did to whatever thought you had.

My idea of mindfulness is consciously putting down my phone and engaging with my son; focusing completely on him and what he wants to do, or just watching him as he builds or colors. I find it soothing to try to see the world through his eyes, instead of my harried, too busy lens.

Meditation

Nowadays, in the age of hustle, it's easy to get lost in the busy-ness of life. But taking the time to slow down and contemplate why you're doing something is a healthy way to look at life.

One way to help with this is meditation.

There is no one way to meditate, but the way that most people think of when they think of meditation is sitting on a floor cross-legged, straight back, hands resting on your knees with palms facing upward or in a chair with your feet planted firmly on the floor.

While this is the traditional way of meditating, I firmly believe that it is personal to you. For me, I sit on my bed or couch, rest my back against the pillows as straight as I can, and sometimes my hands are just resting in my lap. Other times, they are palms up on my legs (I can't quite comfortably reach my knees the way I like to rest while meditating). Other times, I lie down to do it. Whatever tickles my fancy that morning.

Most people tell me they just don't have the time or can't sit still for hours on end to do this. Or that they have a hard time shutting off their brains. I say you don't have time not too. For me, the benefits of it far outweigh not doing it, and I would hazard a guess that if they gave it a chance they would agree.

The point of meditating is not to turn off your brain, that is physically impossible. The brain runs 24/7, even when you sleep, which is why some people say they have a hard time sleeping because their brain just won't stop. The point of meditation is to calm the brain. To recognize the thoughts and to acknowledge them, but to not let them control you anymore, and you don't need hours to do this. You can start small; 10 minutes is all I started with because I felt the same way when it was suggested to me that I try meditating. Slowly over months, I worked my way up to 20 and 30 minutes. After about a year or 18 months, I was finally able to sit for an hour, but realistically I only sit for between 10 - 20 minutes each morning. It's also not about shutting off the brain, it's more about acknowledging the thoughts that you do have and then letting them go instead of focusing on them to the exclusion of all else.

We all have thoughts, it's impossible to shut them off completely, but it is possible to see them and let them move on like clouds in the sky, let them float by. I like to acknowledge them by saying thank you for bringing yourself to my attention, but I'm going to let you go for now. Then I move on to the next one that comes along. Eventually, they don't bother me, and I am able to focus on other things.

One way to do this is with breathwork. Taking lots of deep breaths. Breath in for the count of three or four, hold for four and then breathe out for five. Keep doing this until you feel your brain starts to calm down.

Something else I found helpful was softly staring at a candle. It is almost impossible to think thoughts while staring at a candle. Don't stare right at it but soften your gaze and stare just off to the side or near the bottom. Also, pay attention to your breathing.

However, what I have found most helpful is having some soft music in the background or in my ear pods. Then I can tune out the noise of the world, as I live on a very busy road, for a few minutes and focus on the music to calm myself.

There are some great apps to help you on this journey:

Headspace - This app is free for 10 days and you have a couple of options to start yourself off. Three minute and 10 minutes meditations and the creator Andy Puddicombe walks you through the beginning stages of your meditation journey. After the 10 days, it's a paid app.

Calm - This app has some free options that are good, but to access more it's a paid app as well.

Insight Timer - This is an amazing free app with a paid option if you would like to access various courses, and it's the one that I use the most. There are guided meditations, music meditations, and you have the option of trying out some of the courses for five minutes for free but any longer and you need to pay. There are meditations for a short as one minute up to about 90 minutes.

YouTube - Always free, you can search for all kinds of meditations from Transcendental Meditation (TM), beginner meditation, meditation for sleeping, for relaxing, guided meditation, use your imagination for what to search for and start giving them a try. You won't know what you like until you experiment.

Spotify - This app has a free version and a paid version, search for 'wellness.' Under this heading, there are all kinds of options, yoga, nature sounds, relaxation, meditation, etc. Again, experiment until you find something that works for you.

Over the years I've found out that by implementing a schedule that includes meditation, it has become something I really look forward to. It is a non-negotiable in my mornings. It has also been one of the ways that my brain now figures out problems, ideas, or thoughts that have been elusive. There have been many times when these thoughts or ideas have finally shown themselves to me while I am meditating. I used to just say okay, I see you and thank you, and continue with my practice, but when I came out of the practice, I would have forgotten whatever idea or thought I'd had. Now, I give myself the grace to 'break' the practice to write down these thoughts or ideas and go back into the practice once I've written it down. Giving myself the grace to create a practice that works for me has helped immensely with sleep, overthinking, and stressing about how it's supposed to look a certain way based on research I've done.

As long as you are doing something you enjoy, don't let anyone tell you it should be a certain way. Make it your own and have some fun with it.

Mantras and Affirmations

Mantras and affirmations are just one more way to assist on your journey to shift your thinking, and I feel they go hand in hand with meditating as they can be said silently while meditating. Although in any stressful situation they can be helpful.

I recommend researching and creating mantras and affirmations that will resonate with you on a personal level, but here are some examples that I have used depending on my mood and what issue I was looking to work through or calm down from.

"Today is a good day to have a good day.

With every breath, I feel myself relaxing.

I have control over how I feel, and I choose to feel at peace.

Dear universe/source/God, please grant me "x" or something even greater. Thank you.

There are no mistakes, only lessons to be learned. I have done the best I could.

At this moment in time, I choose to release the past and look forward to the good that awaits.

With every breath, I release the anxiety within me, and I become calmer.

I love myself deeply and unconditionally.

I choose to give myself the same care and attention that I give to others."

I recommend writing them on Post-it notes and placing them strategically around the house, so you always notice them, or as I have done in the past - I got some dry erase markers and wrote them on my bathroom mirror.

Sleep Hygiene

Speaking about sleep hygiene, I mean a variety of practices and habits that are necessary to have good, quality nighttime sleep. This is important for your overall physical health and mental well-being. Having good sleep hygiene can improve your productivity and overall quality of life.

The most important practice of sleep hygiene is to make sure you are getting enough sleep, not too little and not too much. Recommended sleep varies across age groups and is also impacted by lifestyle and health, so be sure to consult a physician or check out our website for ideas on what might be fit you and your lifestyle.

Our brain never shuts off, which is why a night of good sleep is crucial for us as it clears out the toxins that naturally build up throughout the day. There are two types of cells, microglial cells, and astrocytes, that during our sleep cycles clear our brain of these toxins. Microglial cells remove the toxic protein found in our brain called beta-amyloid, which is found in high concentrations in Alzheimer's patients, and the astrocytes clear away any unnecessary synapses and repair our neural wiring.

However, if we are deprived of sleep then these cells not only attack the toxins, but they start to attack our healthy functioning tissue, which can then impair our thinking and emotional regulation.

Sleep disorders were once thought to be a symptom of other psychiatric disorders, such as anxiety and depression, but now doctors are realizing that sleep problems may, in fact, raise the risk for or directly contribute to the development of these disorders, which is why good sleep hygiene practices are so critical.

Good sleep hygiene can foster mental and emotional resilience, while chronic sleep deprivation could set the stage for negative thinking and emotional vulnerability.

There are other good sleep hygiene practices that you can include in your daily routine starting today that will help:

- Limit daytime naps to no more than 20-30 minutes.
- Avoid stimulants such as caffeine and nicotine too close to bedtime.
- Alcohol - although it is known to help with falling asleep faster, consuming alcohol, in general, disrupt your sleep in the latter half of the night when the body starts to process the alcohol.

- Steep clear of fatty, fried, heavy, rich, or spicy foods - these can cause indigestion, which could lead to painful heartburn during the night. It's best to just avoid food, in general, an hour or two before bed so that your body isn't busy working on digesting the food while you sleep.

- Snacking - while a light snack before bed is something I have always grown up doing, I have found that not eating for at least 60 to 90 minutes before bed helps me fall asleep faster, and I don't wake in the night to go to the bathroom; my body has done most of its digestion before I even get into bed.

- Exercising - as little as 10 minutes a day can significantly improve your sleep but it's best to avoid strenuous workouts close to bedtime as the body does need time to relax and cool down before sleep.

- Bedroom - while your pillows and bed itself should be comfortable and inviting, your bedroom should also be kept cool, it's best if you keep blankets on the bed for warmth as opposed to turning the heat on. Consider keeping a window cracked for some fresh air.

- Lights and noises - TVs, traffic, background noise, and the sun can all affect overall sleep. While there is not much that can be done about traffic or how your bedroom is situated with regard to the sun setting, there are ways to minimize these disruptions such as earplugs, white noise machines, blackout curtains, and consider removing the TV from the room to avoid the temptation of turning it on before bedtime.

- Create a bedtime ritual - this will signal to the body that it's time to shut down for the night. Make it as calming as possible and stick to a regular bedtime and morning wake up time, the body likes routine.

If you must eat before bed, make sure it's just a light snack - some peanut butter and apple slices or some avocado toast. It's best to consume the majority of your calories in the earlier part of the day so your body has time to digest everything before you want to go to bed.

If you do suffer from regular wakeups during the night, start to be more conscious of your food choices, maybe a shift in your diet can help eliminate those late night/early morning wake up calls.

Some bad examples of sleep hygiene would be:

- Napping for long periods of time, especially later in the day, anything more than 30 minutes will disrupt your sleep pattern.
- Having a cigarette or caffeine right before bed can stimulate the brain, which can send it into overdrive while trying to fall asleep.
- Snacking right up until bedtime, the body does the majority of its digesting in the early morning hours

- Lying in bed to watch some TV before turning out the light. While a bit of comedy couldn't hurt, a lot of Americans like to sit and catch up on the day's events before bed, but with all the violence in the world today that can stimulate the brain, and if you already worry about various items, watching a burning building or a clip on the war in Syria is not going to make your brain feel better.

It's not just the brain that requires good sleep habits, everything our body needs to repair itself is done while we sleep, which is why developing good sleep habits is crucial. While our brain needs glucose to fuel itself during the day, our digestive tract needs that glucose at night to work its magic. The tissues in this area require the glucose to repair, grow and rebuild themselves and if you eat too large a meal or snack before bedtime then our digestion doesn't have time to rest and repair itself as it is busy breaking down the food you just consumed, which can lead to heartburn or indigestion.

You may find that with less sleep you are prone to more anxious thoughts, to grabbing that sugary snack in the afternoon to get you through. These feelings and thoughts aren't all in your head, they are a biological response to lack of sleep. We are more likely to make poor decisions when running on less sleep, which is why establishing good sleep hygiene practices and routines are so critical to our well-being. One thing with sleep hygiene is quieting the mind. We have been discussing this throughout the book and while it can take time to put all of this into practice, it's critical that you start to find habits that will resonate with you so that you can maintain the practice of no longer overthinking things. Don't think of these in terms of things you 'should' do because at some point you will resent the practice, and it won't maintain it. Think of this in terms of something I 'want' to do. Something that will give me peace of mind. Because then you will want to incorporate it into your day, and the practice will be easier to maintain.

Nighttime can be when the brain will go into overdrive because there is nothing else to distract you from your thoughts, the kids are in bed, work is done for the day, and you can't zone out on the TV or your phone.

One thing that has helped me is keeping a journal and pen beside my bed. Once the brain starts going and the hamster starts up his wheel with things I forgot to do or things I said or didn't say or whatever it is that is keeping me awake, I will sit up and start writing, a big brain dump of all the noise in my head. I have found that the act of pen to paper tells the brain that I have sorted out the problems, and I can either stop worrying about them or I can worry about them another day but not tonight. Tonight, I sleep.

Practice

With all of the technology at our fingertips, it's hard to shut off at times, especially with a lot of our jobs now expecting us to be available 24/7, but it is so important to develop good patterns and habits for good, quality sleep, which is why it's important to develop and establish a relaxing bedtime routine so that you can signify to your body that it's the end of the day.

My two biggest tips for this would be:

Establishing a bedtime routine that you can do regularly and doesn't feel like a chore. Once we feel that something is a chore or we 'have' to do it or it's something we 'should' be doing, we tend to try it a few times and then let it slip. But if we can find something that we enjoy doing and 'want' to do, then it becomes a part of us and our routine and in some cases starts to become a non-negotiable in our life.

So, start to find things that you enjoy doing and can find the time to help your body start to prepare for bedtime. A warm bath or shower, reading a book in bed before lights out, meditating, journaling, or some light stretching. It doesn't matter what you do as long as it's something you want to do and can make a habit out of.

I firmly believe the next critical piece to good sleep hygiene and that is:

Cell phones - TURN THEM OFF!

Today with cell phones being so prevalent, it can be hard to put them down; however, research is showing that these devices are possibly the biggest factor now in sleep disruption. From the blue light they emanate to the pings and beeps of notifications, we are hyper-aware of and connected to our phones. Putting them away an hour or more before bedtime, avoiding any kind of news or social media, and turning off notifications or setting it to airplane mode before bed will help with overall sleep. Consider leaving it in another room, or if it's your alarm clock then leave it across the room, so you have to get out of bed to turn it off. That way, you're not tempted to check it throughout the night, and when it goes off in the morning you have the added benefit of having to get out of bed right away to turn it off, instead of hitting snooze a few times, which also affects our state of mind throughout the day. One last thing about cell phones, also consider not even looking at your phone until you've been awake for an hour or so. If looking at social media or your email is the first thing you do before even getting out of bed, then you're already risking being anxious and depressed and in a negative state before your feet have even touched the floor. Get up, have a shower, have a coffee or some breakfast, chat with your kids, then maybe open up your phone if you have to but not the minute your alarm goes off.

Final Thoughts

Consider this, throughout this book we have talked about intentional thinking, mindfulness, gratitude, meditation, etc. What does it mean to be mentally strong? When you think mentally strong what comes to mind? Because my hope for you with this book is that become mentally strong.

Here are some of my thoughts on the subject:

- Mentally strong people exercise a lot. Thinking of exercise, you probably immediately imagine the impact on the body, but exercising your body also has positive side effects on the brain. But I also think of exercise as engaging in activities that you enjoy, if it´s not an exercise that's fine, just find something you enjoy so you are more likely to keep at it. If it has a physical side to it, even better.

- Mentally strong people believe in socializing and do so as much as they can. When you socialize you are being present and spending less time worrying. Be sure to set some time aside to have some meaningful conversations with friends.

- Mentally strong people understand the need for self-care and looking after themselves. It never falls to the wayside in favor of everyone else's needs.

- Mentally strong people recognize that there will be times of weakness when you'll worry about something and it will consume more time than you would usually spend on an issue. They give themselves the grace to work through it. They may set aside time to think about it and when that time is up, they let it go.

Now I would like to leave you with this one last final thought (I swear it's the last one, really), if at any point throughout this book you've caught yourself saying "Yeah, but" or "I don't have time for this" or "I just can't sit still to meditate," well, let me tell you this, there are no amounts of "Yeah, but's" that should stop you from wanting more peace of mind, you really don't have the time NOT to do any of this for you sanity.

Here is one little item that kind of kickstarted my journey to self-awareness and healing. The rest sort of snowballed after I implemented this into my day.

Monster Under the Bed

We all have those things, that little stories that we tell ourselves every day. Whether they are true or things we have picked up over the years, they are insidious little bits that crop up at the most inopportune times. "I'm not worthy," "I'm not good enough," "I'm not pretty enough," "I'm not rich enough," "I can't do that I'm not smart enough," blah, blah, blah, you are a piece of stardust on earth and an amazing human being. Just somewhere along the way, you were fed some crap and your brain decided to believe it.

Here is what I would like you to try:

In a journal or on some blank paper, I would like to write out at least 10 stories you tell yourself at any given point. If you're on a roll don't stop at 10, keep going, you want to release all the negativity. Because then you are going to SMASH all the negative thoughts.

Now look over the list. Are there any that jump out at you as the ones that seem to run around in your head all day every day? Pick at a minimum of five of these negative statements but try for at least ten of them. Now I want to write the exact opposite of those statements starting with "I am." These will become your new mantra. But we're not stopping here.

Once you have the opposite statements all written out, now I want to grab your phone and record yourself saying these new positive affirmations and repeat them at least five times back to back all in the same recording.

Now comes the really hard part. I want you to listen to this recording every morning for the next few weeks before you even get out of bed or look at social media. This one little thing made me so uncomfortable, but it changed everything for me! I hope it does for you too.

Conclusion

Overthinking doesn't sound any evil on the surface, right? But now you know it can cause various problems. When you overthink, your judgments get obscure and your stress levels rise. You can't spend too much time in the negative, you probably already know very well it's too tricky to act in this state of mind. Let me highlight the major steps you need to follow, the steps you should focus on daily:

1. **The key to self-mastery is self-awareness.**

Before you focus on any of the following, or earlier mentioned practices, you need to learn to be aware of when the overthinking happens. Anytime you catch yourself started thinking about something too much, doubting, feeling worried, stressed or anxious, slow down, realize the situation and look at how you're reacting. That's the crucial moment of awareness, that's the best time for new beginnings.

2. **When you think positive, good things happen.**

Stop being afraid of what could go wrong and start focusing on and being excited about what can go right. For most of the affected people, overthinking is caused by one emotion: fear. It's easy to become paralyzed if you focus on the negatives.

When these thoughts will come to you, stop them at the beginning and imagine ALL the things that can go right, and they really will.

3. Think happy - BE happy

It´s not a cliché, it´s a fact. The state of happiness in whatever form can keep you away enough from overthinking everything. Practice meditation, exercise, find a hobby, let go of what´s gone and be grateful for what remains. Look forward to what´s to come next.

4. Realize the real matter of things

How much will they matter in a few weeks, months, years? Sometimes just this simple question answers and shuts the wiring of your brain off itself.

"The right perspective makes the impossible possible".

5. Don´t wait for perfection.

Being ambitious is great but waiting for perfection is not attainable and is debilitating. Whenever you find yourself waiting for a perfect moment, just take that moment, work hard and make it perfect yourself.

"Waiting for perfect is never as smart as making progress."

6. Don´t worry about the future

Why should you even? Take care of the present, and the future will adjust. You are the one who takes control of your life.

7. Overcome your fears

Think about something that you´re afraid of - for example walking lonely outside in the dark, and beat it slowly every day, step by step. Every night, have a short walk outside in the woods and serve it little by little, adding a few minutes every day.

Consider this fear as an opportunity to improve yourself. Every opportunity is a new beginning - a place to start, reprogram your mind to not to be afraid of your fears.

8. Set limits for thinking

Anytime you really need to think about anything, set a timer for 5 minutes and let yourself analyze it. The other 10 minutes, sit down and write down everything you are worried about, everything that stresses you, get it all out. When the timer goes off, wrinkle the paper and throw it in the bin and bring your thoughts to something more fun.

9. Be grateful

Gratitude is the best medicine. It heals your mind, your body, and your spirit. And attracts more things to be grateful for. Every night and every morning make a list of things you´re grateful for. Keep it in your head or write it down on a paper, if you need to. There´s so much to be grateful for.

10. Accept your best

Overthinking often comes from people's doubts they're not good enough. Not smart enough, not skinny enough, pretty enough. The moment you accept yourself, you grow.

"When you know yourself, you are empowered. When you accept yourself, you are invincible."

— Tina Lifford

Before I go, though, I would like to leave you with this last thought, that overthinking in and of itself is not a bad thing. It's what makes us human, and it's perfectly normal to think about things when it comes to the safety of our family and friends. What isn't normal is having it rule your life.

With deep roots in anxiety and depression, overthinking is an insidious problem that doesn't seem to be going away anytime soon. What we need to work on is giving ourselves the grace to mess up. We have to stop being so hard on ourselves when we make mistakes or aren't the best in the room. In any given situation, there is a good chance there will be others better than us, and we can't beat ourselves up for that. It's a recipe for disaster if we do.

Our mind can run around in circles ad nauseam if we let it, but we need to learn to take back control of our thoughts, learn to be happy, grateful for the things we do have and worry about the things that we can control. By being present, no longer ruminating on the past, and not worrying about what the future brings will help to stop the vicious cycle of overthinking, perfectionism, anxiety, and depression.

I'm not saying this will be easy but learning to be grateful for and appreciate the small AND big things in life will help to rewire the brain into being more positive and stopping the negativity in its tracks. It will also help you live more in the present as there is no time to worry about the past or the future if you are living in the now. I said it earlier, and I think it bears repeating, it is impossible to have negative thoughts and positive thoughts simultaneously, so always choose positive.

Remember your mind is a powerful tool that can be used for destructive or constructive purposes. You can allow it free reign to run amok with unwanted and undesirable thoughts or you can choose more desirable thoughts like joy and gratitude.

Your mind can be your worst enemy or your best friend and avid supporter.

You get to choose!

References

400 Positive Quotes That Will Make Your Day Wonderful. Retrieved 3 November 2019, from **https://wisdomquotes.com/positive-quotes/**

A quote from The Subtle Art of Not Giving an F*ck. Retrieved 2 November 2019, from **https://www.goodreads.com/quotes/8678550-at-some-point-most-of-us-reach-a-place-where**

B., O. 27 Powerful Quotes to Boost Your Self Confidence | Code of Living. Retrieved 1 November 2019, from **https://www.codeofliving.com/27-powerful-quotes-to-boost-your-self-confidence/**

Chua, C. (2019). How to Stop Procrastinating: 11 Practical Ways for Procrastinators. Retrieved 3 November 2019, from **https://www.lifehack.org/articles/featured/11-practical-ways-to-stop-procrastination.html**

Crockett, R. (2019). The Growth Mindset Choice: 10 Fixed Mindset Examples We Can Change. Retrieved 1 November 2019, from **https://www.wabisabilearning.com/blog/fixed-mindset-examples**

Dunn, C. (2019). 10 Things You Can Do to Boost Self-Confidence. Retrieved 3 November 2019, from **https://www.entrepreneur.com/article/281874**

Edberg, H. (2019). 27 Smart and Simple Ways to Motivate Yourself. Retrieved 4 November 2019, from **https://www.positivityblog.com/motivate-yourself/**

Fixed Mindset vs. Growth Mindset: What REALLY Matters for Success. (2019). Retrieved 1 November 2019, from **https://www.developgoodhabits.com/fixed-mindset-vs-growth-mindset/**

Garcy, P. (2015). 9 Reasons You Procrastinate (and 9 Ways to Stop). Retrieved 2 November 2019, from **https://www.psychologytoday.com/us/blog/fearless-you/201506/9-reasons-you-procrastinate-and-9-ways-stop**

Golden Rules of Goal Setting: Five Rules to Set Yourself Up for Success. Retrieved 1 November 2019, from **https://www.mindtools.com/pages/article/newHTE_90.htm**

Griggs, S. (2018). 11 Tips to Master Self-Discipline and Rid Yourself of Bad Habits. Retrieved 2 November 2019, from **https://startupnation.com/start-your-business/tips-self-discipline-bad-habits/**

How to Practice Mindfulness Meditation - Mindful. (2019). Retrieved 4 November 2019, from **https://www.mindful.org/mindfulness-how-to-do-it/**

Klint, L. Learning is living: Making knowledge a priority. Retrieved 1 November 2019, from **https://www.pluralsight.com/blog/career/making-learning-priority**

Loveless, B. 12 Strategies to Motivate Your Child to Learn. Retrieved 2 November 2019, from **https://www.educationcorner.com/motivating-your-child-to-learn.html**

Meah, A. 36 Inspirational Quotes On Self-Discipline | AwakenTheGreatnessWithin. Retrieved 1 November 2019, from **https://www.awakenthegreatnesswithin.com/36-inspirational-quotes-on-self-discipline/**

Morin, A. (2015). 7 Reasons You Need Mental Strength to Be Successful. Retrieved 2 November 2019, from **https://www.success.com/7-reasons-you-need-mental-strength-to-be-successful/**

Patel, D. (2019). 10 Powerful Ways to Master Self-Discipline. Retrieved 1 November 2019, from **https://www.entrepreneur.com/article/287005**

Patel, N. (2016). 7 Brain Hacks to Improve Your Focus at Work. Retrieved 4 November 2019, from **https://www.forbes.com/sites/neilpatel/2016/08/12/7-brain-hacks-to-improve-your-focus-at-work/#509ebdf959a8**

Rice, A. (2006). Urban Dictionary: Scarlett O'Hara. Retrieved 2 November 2019, from **https://www.urbandictionary.com/define.php?term=Scarlett%20O%27Hara**

Ten Ways to Avoid Temptation and Improve Self-Discipline. Retrieved 2 November 2019, from **https://www.equitybank.com/your-life/ten-ways-to-avoid-temptation-and-improve-self-discipline**

Truex, L. (2019). How to Create an Action Plan to Achieve Your Home Business Goals. Retrieved 1 November 2019, from **https://www.thebalancesmb.com/how-to-create-an-action-plan-to-achieve-your-goals-1794129**

What is mental toughness? - Mental Toughness Inc. Retrieved 3 November 2019, from
http://www.mentaltoughnessinc.com/what-is-mental-toughness/

The Psychology Of New Year's Resolutions. Retrieved 2 November 2019, from:
https://www.iflscience.com/brain/psychology-new-year-s-resolutions/

Cherry, Kendra (2019). Why Mindset Matters for Your Success. Retrieved from:
verywell.com/what-is-a-mindset-2795025

Kane, Becky (n.d.). The Science of Analysis Paralysis: How Overthinking Kills Your Productivity & What You Can Do About It. Retrieved from:
doist.com/blog/analysis-paralysis-and-your-productivity

Krauss Whitbourne, Susan (2017). 5 Reasons to Clear the Clutter Out of Your Life. Retrieved from:
https://www.psychologytoday.com/ca/blog/fulfillment-any-age/201705/5-reasons-clear-the-clutter-out-your-life

Blades, Geoff (2017). How To Take Control of Your Thoughts. Retrieved from:
https://medium.com/thrive-global/how-to-take-control-of-your-thoughts-5e2e6a9dc22c

Benefits of Mindfulness (n.d.). Retrieved from:
https://www.helpguide.org/harvard/benefits-of-mindfulness.htm

Holland, Kimberly (2018). Positive Self-Talk: How Talking to Yourself Is a Good Thing. Retrieved from:

https://www.healthline.com/health/positive-self-talk#identify-the-negative

Lucchesi, Emille Le Beau (2019). The Unbearable Heaviness of Clutter. Retrieved from:
https://www.nytimes.com/2019/01/03/well/mind/clutter-stress-procrastination-psychology.html

Morin, Amy (n.d.). 10 Signs You're an Overthinker. Retrieved from:
https://www.inc.com/amy-morin/10-signs-you-think-too-much-and-what-you-can-do-about-it.html

What is Sleep Hygiene? (n.d.). Retrieved from:
https://www.sleepfoundation.org/articles/sleep-hygiene

Turner, Martin & Barker, Jamie (2014). Fight Overthinking, That Destroyer of Decision Making. Retrieved from:
https://www.entrepreneur.com/article/236137

Bernstein, Rebecca (2016). The Mind and Mental Health: How Stress Affects the Brain. Retrieved from:
https://www.tuw.edu/health/how-stress-affects-the-brain/

Segal, Robert MA (2019). Stress Management. Retrieved from:
https://www.helpguide.org/articles/stress/stress-management.htm

Glucose and the Brain: Improving Mental Performance (2013). Retrieved from:
https://www.eufic.org/en/whats-in-food/article/glucose-and-mental-performance

Singh, Marvin MD (2018). The Surprising Link Between Blood Sugar Balance and Anxiety. Retrieved from:

https://www.mindbodygreen.com/articles/how-blood-sugar-is-connected-to-anxiety-stress

Protect Your Brain From Stress (2018). Retrieved from:
https://www.health.harvard.edu/mind-and-mood/protect-your-brain-from-stress

McNaney, Jenna (2015). 5 Benefits We Can Reap From the Power of Visualization Immediately. Retrieved from:
https://www.huffpost.com/entry/5-benefits-we-can-reap-fr_b_6672638?guccounter=1

Holland, Kimberly (2018). Everything You Need to Know About Anxiety. Retrieved from:
https://www.healthline.com/health/anxiety

What Is Tapping and How Can I Start Using It? (n.s.). Retrieved from:
https://www.thetappingsolution.com/what-is-eft-tapping/

Neuro-Linguistic Programming (n.d.). Retrieved from:
https://www.psychologytoday.com/ca/therapy-types/neuro-linguistic-programming-therapy

Trigger (n.d.). Retrieved from:
https://www.goodtherapy.org/blog/psychpedia/trigger

Edberg, Henrik (2017) 7 Destructive Thought Habits That Can Hold You Back From Living a Happier Life. Retrieved from:
https://www.positivityblog.com/destructive-habits/

Kristina, Julia (2015). 9 Destructive Thinking Patterns and How to Change Them. Retrieved from:
https://juliakristina.com/9-destructive-ways-we-think-and-how-to-change-them/

Goldstein, Michele (2019). How to Control Your Thoughts and Be the Master of Your Mind. Retrieved from:
https://www.lifehack.org/articles/lifestyle/how-to-master-your-mind-part-one-whos-running-your-thoughts.html

Robertson, Travis (n.d.). How to Control You Thoughts in 5 Simple Steps. Retrieved from:
https://travisrobertson.com/personal-development/control-your-thoughts/

What Is The Law of Attraction? (n.d.). Retrieved from:
http://www.thelawofattraction.com/what-is-the-law-of-attraction/

Getting Started With Mindfulness (n.d.). Retrieved from:
https://www.mindful.org/meditation/mindfulness-getting-started/

Mindfulness (n.d.). Retrieved from:
https://www.psychologytoday.com/ca/basics/mindfulness

Schmerler, Jennifer (2015). Don't Overthink It, Less Is More When It Comes to Creativity. Retrieved from:
https://www.scientificamerican.com/article/don-t-overthink-it-less-is-more-when-it-comes-to-creativity/

Brandon, John (2019). Science Says There's a Simple Reason You Keep Thinking Negative Thoughts All Day. Retrieved from:
https://www.inc.com/john-brandon/science-says-theres-a-simple-reason-you-keep-thinking-negative-thoughts-all-day.html

Zimmerman, Angelina (n.d.). The 9 Daily Steps Guaranteed to Shift Your Mindset. Retrieved from:

https://www.inc.com/angelina-zimmerman/10-magnificent-ways-to-master-your-mindset.html

How Digestion Affects Your Sleep Quality (n.d.). Retrieved from:
https://www.sleepadvisor.org/sleep-and-digestion/

Gratitude (n.d.) Retrieved from:
https://www.psychologytoday.com/ca/basics/gratitude

Fader, Sarah (2019). What is Overthinking Disorder? Retrieved from:
https://www.betterhelp.com/advice/personality-disorders/what-is-overthinking-disorder/

Krakovsky, Marina (2011). Field Guide to the Maximizer. Retrieved from:
https://www.psychologytoday.com/ca/articles/201109/field-guide-the-maximizer

Daskal, Lolly (2016). 10 Simple Ways You Can Stop Yourself From Overthinking. Retrieved from:
https://www.inc.com/lolly-daskal/10-simple-ways-you-can-stop-yourself-from-overthinking.html

Printed in Great Britain
by Amazon